In Short: Successful Investing
During Turbulent Times

In Short: Successful Investing During Turbulent Times

LARRY SHORT

iUniverse, Inc.
Bloomington

IN SHORT: SUCCESSFUL INVESTING DURING TURBULENT TIMES

iUniverse books may be ordered through booksellers or by contacting:

iUniverse
1663 Liberty Drive
Bloomington, IN 47403
www.iuniverse.com
1-800-Authors (1-800-288-4677)

ISBN: 978-1-4620-5835-8 (sc)
ISBN: 978-1-4620-6886-9 (ebk)

Printed in the United States of America

iUniverse rev. date: 02/09/2012

Dedication

To Carter–the Football, the Doodle, Dickey-Doo and Poodle.

The many nicknamed boy whose love and laughter energizes everyone around him and inspires his family in so many ways.

Contents

About the Author.. xi

Preface   You Are Not Alone xiii

1. Meetings With Remarkable Clients 1

2. Wisdom vs. Knowledge 14

3. The Parable of the Stutterer:
    Making the Most of a Handicap................................. 20

4. Of Two Minds About Investing................................... 23

5. A Brief History of Time in the Market:
    How Investors and Advisors Reacted........................ 31

6. Consensus is Your Enemy 89

7. The Problem with Financial Plans and the
    Mountain Valley Wealth Management Solution........ 95

8. The Problem with Modern Portfolio Theory............ 100

9. Modern Portfolio Theory Results.............................112

10. An Additional Problem—The Nifty 44:
    The Hollowing Out of the Toronto Stock Exchange 127

11. The Death of Buy and Hold? 131

12. Who's Afraid of a Recession? 136

13. How to Read a Mutual Fund Ad: (Hint—the
    smaller the letters the bigger the message) 143

14. How Your Investment Advisor Gets Paid
    Now and How Much Mutual Funds Cost 147

15. How Your Investment Advisor Will be Paid
    in the Future and How Mutual Fund Fees
    Will be Disclosed In the Future 151

16. How to Choose a Financial Advisor 155

17. Solution One: Becoming a Contrarian 166

18. Solution Two: Fixing Modern Portfolio Theory 168

19. Solution Three:The Value Manager and the
    Concentrated Portfolio 173

20. How to Deal with Inheriting Money,
    Selling a Business or Winning a Lottery 184

21. The Lesson of the Boy Who Cried Wolf 195

22. The Next Roller Coaster Ride 198

    Appendix A   The True Cost of Fund Ownership 205

    Glossary 211

Author's Note

This publication is solely the work of Larry Short. Although the author is a registered Investment Advisor with DWM Securities Inc., a DundeeWealth Inc. Company, this is not an official publication of DWM Securities Inc. The views (including any recommendations) expressed in this book are those of the author alone, and they have not been approved by, and are not necessarily those of, DWM Securities Inc.

Readers are specifically advised that this book contains general information for educational purposes and under no circumstances should be considered as specific investment advice. Readers should seek investment advice suitable to their specific circumstances from an investment professional before making any investment decisions.

About the Author

Larry Short was born and raised in Carbonear, Newfoundland and Labrador. He attended Memorial University of Newfoundland and graduated in 1981 with a Bachelor of Commerce (B.Comm) degree.

He worked as a manager in the Finance department of Newfoundland Telephone for a number of years while studying to attain his Certified General Accountant (CGA) designation.

In 1988 he began working as an Investment Advisor at RBC Dominion Securities.

He was actively involved in the community and had numerous volunteer positions including Chairing the Board of Directors of the Newfoundland Symphony Orchestra, where he met his later-to-be wife, Kimberley.

Larry moved to TD Waterhouse in 2002 as Senior Investment Advisor and Vice President.

In 2008, wanting to make a fundamental change in his wealth management practice, Larry and his team moved to DundeeWealth.

Over the years Larry has worked and achieved numerous professional designations aside from his B. Comm and CGA. Larry is a Certified Financial Planning (CFP®) Professional, a Certified Investment Manager (CIM), as well as a Portfolio Manager. Larry's commitment to continuing education continues to serve his practice and his clients well.

Larry is a published author of *In Short: Secrets to Make Your Dollars Grow* (Doubleday 1998), and has been featured on local and national radio and television. Larry hosts several client education and appreciation events each year, including: *Women and Wealth (2005-2007), Tax Reduction Strategies for Business Owners and Professionals (2006-onward), Succession Planning for Business Owners (2007-2008), and When Will the Recession End, Preparing to Prosper (2009).*

Larry's wealth management practice is with DundeeWealth in St. John's, Newfoundland & Labrador.

Preface

You Are Not Alone

As investors, many of you have done all the things that you were supposed to do and you are frustrated because you have not been able to achieve the desired results. That is, you have hired reputable, sincere, knowledgeable professional money managers and investment advisors who have placed you into "top performing", "first quartile" and "five star" funds or with individual managers, but over the years your investment results have been disappointing. Or, you have done this work on your own using a discount service and have still not achieved your goals.

As advisors, many of us have done exactly what we were told we should do: we have listened to the experts, placed our clients' money with "professional investment managers" and mutual funds with the clients' best interests in mind and had to express regret to the clients because time and time again their investment returns have been so disappointing.

And investing in the stock market since 1998 looks more like a roller coaster ride than at any other time. It may very well be that this pattern will continue in the future and that we have indeed entered an era of roller coaster style returns. So poor had investing results become in 2008 and 2009 that noted consultant to the investment industry, Bill Good, started calling investment advisors "professional apologists" because, for the third time in ten years (1998, 2000-2003, and 2008), advisors had to tell clients they were sorry that investment returns had been disastrously reduced during the latest market crash.

It was one thing to have the crash of 1998 scare people around the world as banks fell and Long Term Capital Management, an investment firm run by two Nobel Prize in Economics winning geniuses, failed and almost took western society with it. It was another to have the high tech bubble collapse in 2000 and wipe out trillions of dollars of investors' savings. But to have a third market tragedy in ten years in 2008 on our watch was, in many clients' minds, inexcusable. After all, we have 24 hour surveillance of economic events and modern computerized communication, not to mention the highest educated and smartest analysts on staff and the ability to swiftly move clients' money out of the market. How could such a huge problem with the world's financial system be missed by so many bright minds? How could we not know we were again in a bubble?

How many times can an advisor tell a client that the methods the investment industry employs are sound, that the processes are the best and that the professionals they hired indeed do know what they are doing—how can we sound knowledgeable and trustworthy when clients' life savings fall as dramatically as they have three times in ten years?

No wonder we are sometimes called professional apologists.

Something has to change. There has to be a better solution for these turbulent times.

But it is more than "just" the advisors who have a problem, or the clients or the methodologies individually. It is the combination of all three that has to be addressed.

So, whether you are an investor or an advisor, I can tell you that you are not alone.

In addition to this call to action, we are also on the cusp of major and dramatic changes to the investment industry around the world, including here in Canada. These changes will affect the investor as well as the investment advisory firms and their employees. It will be more important than ever that you be aware of the upcoming changes because it will make for a different, and hopefully better, investment experience.

To begin, let us break these issues down into its components.

Let us start with recognizing the problems with the long-term returns that investors have been earning over the years.

Chapter 1

Meetings With Remarkable Clients

In May 2008, the Toronto stock market reached an all time high and there was much anticipation with what promised to be a wonderful summer. However, a conversation with one of my oldest and wisest clients disturbed me. This remarkable gentleman, who is in his 70's, and I had been working together for many years with me picking his brain about the stock market, interest rates, bonds and mutual funds and then collectively coming to a decision as to what and how to invest in his account. I know it is supposed to work the other way around with him asking me questions. Afterall, I was the one with all the book learnin', the degrees and designations, but this client is one of a cherished, rare breed who has been investing for a long time, who has seen the soaring and crashes of past markets well before I came into the business.

We spoke quarterly on a scheduled call basis and during this call he reminded me that the last time that the price of oil tripled, which was in 1973, the stock markets around the world had crashed shortly after. Well, here we were in 2008 with markets at all time highs and the price of oil had tripled from recent times. He was worried and when he worried, it portended trouble.

I asked him what he wanted to do. He said "Raise the stop loss orders on my individual stocks". I asked him what he wanted done on the money in his mutual funds. He explained that he was satisfied that the mutual fund manager would take the appropriate action if the market did indeed fall.

Shortly after, the Toronto stock market did peak and fall and his stocks were stopped out (the stop loss orders were triggered and the stocks sold). He was now in cash as the markets fell through August and all the way down to January 2009.

We were in contact during that period with discussions on the markets and interest rates.

Remember, in January of 2009 newspaper headlines were screaming about how terrible the markets were, how the Toronto stock market index had fallen from 15,400 down to below 8,000, how much further we were destined to fall, and how people were selling out of their investments. Canadian bank stocks had fallen over 50% in most cases and panic was very much in the air. One client had told us that their friend was now selling out of his RRSP's "cause they had gone down" and the friend was recommending others do the same.

Later in the book I will explain in more detail that I am a Contrarian investment advisor. This does not mean that my wife and friends think that I am difficult to get along with (that is a very different book). It does mean that I invest in a manner that is generally opposite to the way that most in the investment industry recommend.

One of the reasons for this approach is the wisdom of some of the remarkable clients that I have.

In January of 2009 I again spoke with my long standing client and I presented him with research that showed that the markets were finally bottoming. He agreed. I then started investing his, and other clients', money, back into the stock market, highlighting what I thought were undervalued sectors. I also launched an investment seminar called *"When Will the Recession End: Preparing to Prosper"* advocating that investors start preparing for the end of the recession and position their investments to prosper in the coming months and years.

To say that at least some of the invitees to these seminars thought I was daft is an understatement. In January 2009 almost no one was talking about "prospering". Most investors and advisors were just hoping to survive. And, because the market continued to fall through late January to March, our credibility during those months was heavily questioned.

Being early is always a risk but being late is even more dangerous.

The Toronto stock market bottomed on March 8, 2009 and has soared since (up to time of writing). Those investors that did choose to put money into the market when it appeared to be at its worse have done terrifically well. But most Canadians did not buy during this time. In fact, only 13% of Canadian investors put money in when the market was down. Many more sold out.

In May 2009, I once again spoke with my remarkable client on his scheduled quarterly call. He reminded me how we had sold out of the market in the summer of 2008 and, although we had not sold out at the top, we had sold quite profitably, stayed in cash during the market decline and bought back in somewhere near the bottom. Overall, despite the fact that the stock market was still down, he was ahead of where he was in May 2008 on the money we were managing together.

However his mutual fund manager had not sold anywhere near the top, had not bought during the downturn or at the bottom and the client's investment in the mutual fund was still down significantly. He wanted me to call and ask the fund manager why he was paying a 2.5% management fee for such results. Here was a wise and experienced investor frustrated by his investment and asking a basic question of our industry.

Thus began this interesting trek, hopefully one that you will find beneficial and entertaining.

The answers to his questions were surprising and more multifaceted than at first thought. As my team and I dug deeper into the issues he raised, the findings started to paint a picture of the industry different from what many investors (and their advisors) currently realize.

As my team and I were talking about these issues we found many other writers and researchers going down the same path and I reference them in this book as well.

Taking you on this exploration will help you make sense of why your investments have performed as they have in the past and provide you with the tools to earn better investment results in the future.

Several organizations have been studying investor results for many years. One of the better known industry-recognized studies is one prepared by a company named Dalbar out of the United States. The study is called *The Results of Investor Behaviour* and it compares how much the average investor earns on their mutual funds versus how much the average mutual fund earned in the market.

The study covering the period from 1984 to 2003 showed that the average equity fund in the US rose by 11.5% per year. However, the average investor in equity mutual funds only earned 3.5% per year.

Another way to look at this is that $1,000 invested in the average mutual fund in 1984 grew to $8,821 for the period ended in 2003 for a profit of $7,821. However, the average investor who invested $1,000 only grew their money to $1,990 earning $990 in growth during the same period.

Now you can see that you are really not alone and that this is a wide-spread problem.

How is it possible that investors earned less than their underlying investment? It turns out that investors bought into a mutual fund only after a fund had risen significantly and sold after the fund had fallen.

Illustration 1: Gain on $1000 Invested in 1984

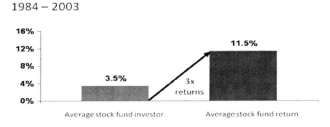

RESULTS OF INVESTOR BEHAVIOUR

1984 – 2003

Illustration 2: Percentage Gain on $1000 Invested in 1984

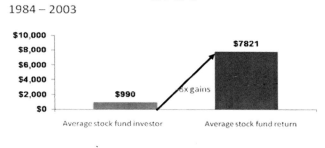

GAIN ON $1000 INVESTED IN 1984
1984 – 2003

Sources: Dalbar Inc. and Lipper Inc.

This is US data. We do not have studies like this for Canadians but there is clear evidence of similar behaviour by Americans and Canadians, so there is no reason to think that results north of the border are any different.

To be clear, this study shows that investors in the US are not earning the returns that the average mutual fund in the US is generating and we can extrapolate that Canadian investor returns are similar.

This problem is not isolated to only the period from 1984 to 2003. This study has been repeated every year since 1984 (i.e. 1985-2004, 1986-2005, 1987-2006, etc . . .) and the results have been the same. Investors have never done as well as their investments.

This is clearly a consumer behaviour problem. After all, the product seems to work fine but the consumers are buying it at the wrong time and selling it at the wrong time. Many advisors have stated that the solution to this problem is to put investors in a series of investments and keep them there forever. This is called the "Buy and Hold" solution and based on Illustrations 1 & 2 this solution seems to have merit. If only investing was that simple.

Later we will see why this solution does not work, but for now I really want to focus on why the average investor is behaving as they do. The dogma of our industry is "buy low, sell high" so why are investors not doing that?

Remember, I stated that this problem is not isolated to the investors themselves. Investors are not alone in making their investment decisions. The investment advisors themselves, the analysts and other industry participants are also involved, particularly in Canada, and the behaviour and recommendations of these additional players directly influence the decisions that Canadian investors make. We will see evidence of all industry participants' behaviour later when we review newspaper headlines during market peaks and crashes.

But to begin, it is vital that you understand how the investment advice industry is set up now, even though it is about to change dramatically.

The best characterization of our industry I have ever found was made by Anthony Boeckh in his book "The Great Reflation" (John Wiley and Sons, 2010) when he wrote:

"It must constantly be kept in mind that Wall Street is a sophisticated manufacturing and marketing machine that will always have unlimited products to sell you (the investor) with the primary motivation being to maximize the bonuses of Wall Street salespeople and the share prices of

Wall Street firms, not the wealth of investors." (The Great Reflation, page 171)

Of course, Bay Street in Canada and the other financial centers around the world are no different than Wall Street. These financial centers are all part of the great "marketing machine". Let me illustrate by telling you about a breakfast meeting I had with one of my mutual fund company contacts late in the summer of 2010.

I need to backtrack a bit—understand that my office receives many solicitations daily for my team to place our clients' money with various mutual fund companies. When a new assistant first joined my practice some years ago she received a phone call from a mutual fund company representative who said he was calling to book a lunch meeting with me. She asked how he knew me. He said he was a wholesaler for a mutual fund company that I had met with before. She said "Wholesaler? What are you selling?" He replied "Our mutual funds."

It had never occurred to this new assistant that a firm providing investment advice would be selling mutual funds. She thought that an investment firm would be providing investment advice but selling always struck her as an activity that requires the customer to be persuaded to buy. She thought that providing investment advice was a service delivered in an unbiased fashion in the best interests of the client, but to be sold something was an action that benefited the seller more than the buyer.

Although a lot of investment advisors have fancy titles such as Vice President or Director, Private Client Group (my title) their success is mostly measured by revenue goals. This can lead to situations where advisors indeed can be tempted to sell something that is more beneficial to himself or herself than to the client.

Let me be clear—the ethical standards in our industry require us to place our clients' interest before our own. Most advisors that I have had the pleasure of knowing are good, honest people with their clients' best interests in the forefront, balancing this with the demands from their employer. This is not an easy job.

I hope that it does not come as a shock to you, though, to read that information from salespeople is often biased. This is not necessarily intentional misrepresentation. More often than not it is a case of a salesperson providing the most favourable interpretation for their mutual fund. After all, how long would a mutual fund salesperson continue to be employed if they told their company's customers to go across the street to buy the competition's fund because it was better?

Let me give you one more example.

You often see advertisements for mutual funds stating that a particular fund has earned superior returns for the last five years. Therefore it seems that buying such a fund is a wise thing to do. The reality is that the track record of the fund has no bearing on what you will earn. It even says so in the fine print of the ad. So why do such ads exist? Because they sell funds.

Having said all of this let's go back to the wholesaler in the summer of 2010. This person had the requisite official title plus the proper degrees and designations behind their name. I asked what they were recommending. The answer was "long term bond funds".

I was shocked.

Long term bond funds obviously invest in long term bonds. These bonds mature 20 to 30 years out and are issued by corporations and governments. They can be bought or sold at any time subject to market prices. One of the biggest factors affecting market prices is the level of long term interest rates. When interest rates are high, like in 1981 when interest rates were 18% in Canada, bond prices are low and you want to buy when prices are low. But when interest rates are low, such as they were in the summer of 2010, bond prices are high. In fact these bonds were at all time record highs and if interest rates rose, which we expected them to, those high bond prices would fall, creating losses for bond investors.

After considerable discussion I asked why I should recommend to our clients that we buy their bond fund. The reply was "It's an easy sell".

What was meant is that if other advisors are buying a particular type of fund at that point in time (which they were), the five year track record for that type of fund looked great (which it did), and the industry as a whole was actively advertising these investments (which it was), then it would be easy to sell the investment to investors. In the summer of 2010 more investors bought more long term bond funds than any other time in history.

So, the wholesaler was right. It was easy to sell it. Whether the clients would make money on it was what I questioned.

And this conversation was not held with only one mutual fund wholesaler—it was held with many that summer. In addition to the direct conversations, there were emails recommending various bond funds, advertisements about "five star" and "top performing" bond funds, new bond issues launched and new bond funds manufactured from many mutual fund companies.

And all this promotion was supported by analysts, wholesalers, and advisors. So you can see how investor behaviour is influenced by what these salespeople promote.

Now that you have a better understanding of how our industry is set up, and how skeptical I am, let's discuss how to make better investment decisions.

In my previous book "In Short: Secrets to Make Your Dollars Grow" (DoubleDay, 1998) I discussed the tools and jargon of the investment industry. You could kind of draw a parallel to that book and say it was a mechanic's manual for an automobile. Staying with the analogy, consider this book as one that teaches you how to drive.

Just look back to the year 1999 when discount firms first enabled the average investor access to the market cheaply and threw in analysis systems including trading maps and charting programs. These are the tools to invest. There arose a group of these amateurs who became known as Day Traders because they were buying in the morning and selling in the afternoon. But this was the time when the high tech market was rising dramatically and almost everything rose so the Day Traders were initially very encouraged.

Then the market peaked in the year 2000 and fell dramatically and many a Day Trader was wiped out. These investors were given the tools to invest but not the knowledge of how to invest.

We will go through a number of lessons in the following chapters. One of the core discussions involves newspaper headlines and articles. My attempt is not to criticize newspapers or the authors of these various articles. It is really easy in this business to look back on investment articles with perfect hindsight and criticize the writer at the time. That is not what I am attempting to do here. I am using these articles as a written record of significant market events and the thoughts of reporters. Most importantly—these reporters were reporting what the analysts and investors were thinking at the time.

Seeing the image of the articles published during key times during a market collapse or during a market bubble places you in the mindset of an investor at the time. This is precious. This is raw data, written on the spot and not tainted by subsequent edits.

The irony is that experience is what you gain by making the wrong decisions. I stand today acknowledging that I have a lot of experience. I have never met a perfect investor or a perfect investment advisor. I have met great investors and incredible investment advisors, several in my hometown, and they all got their wisdom through making mistakes and learning the lessons of experience.

This book is an attempt to provide you with the experience needed to cope with the changing world of investments, to help you prepare for the next market crash, and the opportunities that will arise, by witnessing the mistakes that others, including me, have already experienced. This has to be better than you going through these errors yourself.

So this book is about providing you this needed experience by re-living, or depending on your age, by living through periods when markets surged and when markets collapsed.

There is some repetition, and it is intentional. I have found that when I repeat a lesson in a slightly different way it tends to stick with the reader a bit more.

I have also used relatively old data in a number of circumstances and again it is intentional. I want to show that the problems we discuss today are not new. We have known about many of them for years. Unfortunately, for a long time we could not solve these problems without incurring prohibitive costs, but new techniques and new investment tools allow us to address these problems better now.

We will also journey into the psychology of investing and the argument over whether Modern Portfolio Theory is valid. Modern Portfolio Theory is the paradigm that the industry has been using to "correctly" advise clients. Every investment advisor must know the details and applications of this theory in sufficient detail in order to pass the licensing exams in our industry.

We will talk about whether you should be following this theory and look at alternatives.

Then we will delve into how your investment advisor is paid now and how your advisor will be paid in the future.

Finally, we will address some key factors related to the future of investing and summarize the impact of the various topics on these coming years.

Chapter 2

Wisdom vs. Knowledge

Everyone would like to have instant wisdom but, unfortunately, you can only obtain wisdom through experience and usually, the best experience is obtained through making mistakes and learning from bad decisions.

Most people buy an investment book in hopes of lessening their worry about money. Money is a tool that can allow for great joy and pleasure in life.

Over time worrying about money causes significant and detrimental changes to a person's physical and mental well-being. It literally changes your body and your personality.

And worrying about money is a full time job. In a poll completed by Gallup in the US in 2003, 60% of those asked said that they were worried about their retirement. More recently, another Gallup poll showed that 47% of Americans worried about money on that day.

There are no readily available statistics for Canadians but we are not such a distinct society as to think we are that different from Americans in the worry department.

Unfortunately, most investment books attempt to address worry through the logical presentation of knowledge, but knowledge alone does not help as much as one would think. There are many thousands of graduates coming out of business schools every year who have MBA's, PhD's in Business and CFA's (Chartered Financial Analyst) degrees and designations. I have a few letters behind my name but this book-learnin' does not amount to much if results are not achieved. Without results, book-learnin' really means only that I can read and remember enough of what I have read to reproduce it on paper later.

If knowledge was all we needed, I have little doubt that there would be many more millionaires in your community. But facts and logic (knowledge) are diminished in the face of fear and greed, lost in the sea of despair as well as in a period of elation, and devoid of any aspect of instinct. This is why you need experience.

There is very strong evidence that investors are not logical at all, at least not during periods of worry or elation. We may say "buy low, sell high" but as you will see throughout the book, there is very good evidence that investors do not follow that rule at all. Instead investors cycle back and forth between fear and greed.

On the greed side, investors tend to buy into equity mutual funds (ones that invest in stocks as opposed to bond mutual funds that invest in bonds) and other stock market investments when the level of optimism is highest and tend to sell (fear driven) when pessimism is extreme. Of course these are the worst times to buy and sell, and it explains a lot about how one could be earning a return on an equity mutual fund that is less than what the equity mutual fund itself is earning. The average investor purchases the fund when they should be selling and selling when they should be buying.

We see this in the flow of money into and out of mutual funds over the years. In years after the stock markets have gone up tremendous amounts of money flow into stock market based mutual funds.

Similarly, money comes out of the stock market (investors sell their equity mutual funds) after the stock market has fallen.

And this is not only true for just stock market mutual funds. The same holds for bond funds. That is, investors purchase bond funds only after bond funds have risen and sell them after they have fallen.

This is despite all those thousands of advisors working for great firms who employ educated and accredited analysts who combine their knowledge, complete their economic studies, present their research reports and use only the top funds and the best money managers with all that book-learnin'. This record of actual performance, laid bare and plain for all to see, is not wisdom in action.

But this record of actual investor behaviour goes a long way to explaining your frustration.

If applied knowledge from the extremely well educated pool of advisors, analysts and firm strategists, who are some of the smartest people on the planet, is not explaining why investors are buying and selling in this fashion, then some other factor or factors must be causing investors to behave in this manner.

There are two basic causes of such behaviour.

The first is that investors are not following their advisors' recommendations.

The second is that the advisors' book-learnin' is wrong.

So, let's start with the first question—investors should be logically following their advisors advice. But, what if investors are not logical, or indeed if advisors, analysts, economists, strategists, news commentators, and everyone else involved in the industry are not logical either.

It turns out that, in real life, we are fundamentally emotional beings, secondly we are tribal and, continuing on that path, third, we are subject to the herd mentality. Logic only factors in to any degree when we are under a condition of low stress and when we can take the time to think rationally. Market peaks and troughs, bubbles and irrational exuberance, as well as crashes and plunges are the times most investors and their advisors make their most important decisions. These are all periods of high stress.

Or at least perceived high stress because how you view the investment climate determines whether you are stressed or not.

So, one of the keys to investing successfully may therefore be to invest when you are under low stress conditions. We cannot prevent bubbles and crashes but we can change how you view them.

Insight into stress came to me recently when I experienced one of the highest stress conditions ever in my life while on vacation. I was at Disney World in Florida with my wife and five year old son. My son loves dinosaurs—all types and manner of dinosaur but he is most fond of the meanest of these beasts, those being the Tyrannosaurus Rex and its immediate cousins.

Disney has a ride featuring such dinosaurs. Naturally, my five year old wanted to go on it. Naturally I agreed because of all the other rides that he had been on, none had scared him and none had scared me.

This did.

Like nothing else.

Everything paled by comparison. I really thought I had encountered fear before and although the logical part of my brain knew that the ride was just a ride, the ride designers at Disney found all the buttons to push to override the logic center in my brain, including using shadows and darkness, the noise of being followed, and unexpected screams from various directions to move my adrenalin to hyper drive and cause me to consider the survival of my son as the only task of importance. Time dilation took place—the few minutes on that ride seemed to last for hours.

I am not sure how scared the other people on the ride were. I am certain they would have been much more scared if they knew that at one point I was mentally calculating which of them I could throw off the ride and in what order to feed the pseudo dinosaurs in the hope of slowing the beasts down so my son would survive.

The bottom line is that, despite all the supposed advances in civilization over the centuries, our bodies still retain the reflexes that kept us alive in the caveman days.

Such insight, in these extreme conditions, helped me realize what many investors go through during a market crash. Although the duration of the crash may be longer, it causes similar illogical decisions. What these investors throw to the beasts, though, is not their neighbours but their investments.

Here is the other part of the lesson—if I went back on the same ride I would not have been as scared. Repeating the ride makes the ride less scary to the point of finally being boring. If you know how the ride proceeds, if you become familiar with the ups and downs enough to start to expect them, and if you have been through enough times to know how it ends, then stress dissipates.

That is the point where wisdom has been obtained.

This also applies to investing. Once you realize this fully you can start to understand the decision making processes that you go through and begin to accept and overcome the reflex nature of your emotions. We next discuss a handicap most people are born with, one that you most likely not even aware of.

Chapter 3

The Parable of the Stutterer:
Making the Most of a Handicap

Years ago I heard the story of a man living in the US Deep South where the Southern drawl drags out sentences into paragraphs and paragraphs into encyclopedias. Let's call him Elroy, not an uncommon name in the area at the time.

This unfortunate chap lived during one of the worst of times—the Great Depression—and was further encumbered by a very pronounced stutter.

One can imagine how your heart would go out to Elroy and you would not be surprised to learn that this individual had a difficult time trying to earn a wage, despite having a keen and intelligent mind.

You may be surprised to learn that when Elroy saw the advertisement of a bible supplier coming to town looking for salesmen to sell bibles door to door, he knew he had met his means to wealth creation and a lifetime of worry free income.

Consider that the bible supplier has 50 books per case selling at $1 per bible. Sales are on a consignment basis only, meaning that the salesman only gets paid if he sells the bibles but the supplier also only gets paid when the salesman comes back with cash and has invested in buying the books himself so he has the additional cost of carrying the inventory as well as the possibility that the bibles may never get sold. As the supplier, one would only want to invest in the best salesmen around.

After meeting with a number of salesmen who are well spoken and mannerly and used to rejection, and therefore properly prepared for the difficulty of door to door sales in a terrible time in an onerous place, the supplier encounters Elroy, the man with the stutter.

Gut feel immediately tells him that this person will never sell bibles, or anything else door to door for that matter. The glint in Elroy's eye belies his first impression and Elroy's persistence causes the supplier to either trust him or simply to give up.

In the end, it may have been the stutter. Regardless, the supplier gives the man 50 books, some instructions and tells him to bring back the books or the money in five days. He thinks there is a high probability that he will never see the books or the person again.

Three hours later, Elroy appears looking relaxed and refreshed and passes over the $50 with the ease and grace of a fine southern gentleman. The bible supplier is shocked and amazed and suddenly realizes that he has been replaced as being the all time top salesman for the firm by this surprising young man and demands to know how 50 bibles were sold in three hours.

Elroy calmly picks up a bible, mimics knocking on a door and begins his script:

"Good afternoon Sir or Maam" which really came out as "Gooood Af-terrrnnnnnnononoon Siiiiir or or or

Maa—aa—ammm" and proceeded to stutter through his introduction to point out that he had a perfectly good bible in front of himself here that the Sir or Mam could buy or "I c-c-c-could r-r-r-r-r-r-read it to you!"

Here was a man who was fully aware of having a handicap and employed that awareness to the best of his ability to not only overcome it but to employ it to better himself and his family.

It has been my observation that most of us are Elroys when it comes to investing but in our case we have a handicap we are not aware of. Now that we recognize it let's call it the Great Handicap. Recognizing that we have the problem is the first step. Overcoming it will make a great difference in your life.

Now, let's get a better handle of what I mean by being emotional, tribal and subject to the herd mentality.

Chapter 4

Of Two Minds About Investing

Most people start out having two minds about investing their own money for one simple reason—we indeed are all born with at least two brains. The Great Handicap I alluded to in the previous chapter is that we are not aware of how we truly make decisions.

We would all like to think that we have one logical, "in control" mind. But a number of researchers over the years have revealed that the mind we logically think with is a relatively slow, logical mind. Make no mistake—I am talking about the one often thought to "reside" behind our eyes which is also the one you are reading this book with.

Our second, more powerful and much faster processing mind is our intuitive center that I call the "gut feel" because it "resides" in one's belly.

The gut feel brain is also discussed in a book called *Blink* (Back Bay Books, Little, Brown, 2005). I urge you to read it in its entirety. Here are three examples from the book.

1) University students were shown a 0.5 second tape (yes that was half of one second) of a university professor speaking with students. They were then asked to rate

the professor on a series of items including likeability, communications skills, ease of approach etc. They then compared the results of the 0.5 second sample to the survey done by students who were taught by him for 13 weeks. Here's the kicker—the survey results were identical. That is, the students with the 0.5 second sample correctly perceived the professor to have the same attributes as the students exposed to the 13 week course.

2) An insurance company in the US who insured doctors against malpractice began to employ a similar approach whereby the assessors viewed a 0.5 second sample of the doctor speaking with patients and then rated them on the likelihood of the doctor being sued successfully in the future. Some years later they then reviewed the actual legal history of these same doctors. They found that their predictability was incredibly accurate.

3) In both cases, subsequent studies garbled the 0.5 second sample so that no words could be made out or tone of voice detected. Results were still consistent.

Further, in another piece of research "micro facial expressions" have been discovered by a chap named Paul Ekman, a professor of psychology at the University of Southern California.

Apparently, he "has identified and isolated specific and sometimes involuntary movements of the 44 human facial muscles linked to fear, distrust, distress and other emotions related to deception." He calls the micro expressions "emotional leakage" that signals when a person is willfully or unconsciously trying to suppress an emotion. His book, *Emotions Revealed* (Henry Holt and Company, 2007) details his findings in full.

Although he states that 80% to 90% of people he tested do not recognize these expressions in other people, I would suggest that we humans have been detecting such negative and positive micro expressions subconsciously for years. (His book claims to teach people how to recognize these expressions consciously.)

Such is the importance and subtlety of these micro-expressions that the expressions are being deliberately programmed into robots to make them more acceptable to humans.

The discussion of multiple brains or processing centers was also picked up by Nassim Nichalols Taleb in his book *Fooled by Randomness* (Random House, 2001).

This is a book that I could quote from on a number of topics and, although some friends and clients have found to be too dry a read, I urge you to add it to your collection of must reads.

Taleb goes into the multiple brain theory and documents various researchers and their explorations. He then condemns journalists and writers who overly simplify the theories in order to condense this fascinating area of research into a sound bite.

Perhaps I am not doing justice to the complexity of his theory, however, I am going to simplify it for you.

The point of proposing the theory of two minds is to help explain why investors are naturally prone to making investment mistakes. Here is my oversimplified explanation:

The intuitive, gut feel, brain has been evolving ever since we emerged as humans, which was supposedly some 30 million years ago. The intuitive mind has been called the fast thinking mind. This fast thinking part of our anatomy helped determine which humans survived to produce more children and natural selection ruled out those who did not develop this skill. Such intuitive processing determined when to flee or fight and through detection of micro-facial expressions, who to trust, who to mate with, and who to believe. There is evidence that we also pick up trace elements of odours, such as pheromones and this is another factor that also feeds into the gut feel brain.

So, consider that some 15 thousand years ago, a hunting party you are part of observes a large, hairy beast, say, a giant short faced bear, fall from a tree in front of you.

(The short faced bear is known as Arctodus Simus and was the largest land carnivore within the last 20,000 years. Think of something the size of a polar bear but a much faster runner. Such things as nightmares are made of . . .)

You, as an individual, have a fraction of a second to decide whether this is an opportunity or a threat. Is the animal wounded or ready to pounce? If you stay and fight, who will stay with you? (micro expression reading.) Are there relatives (children) in the group that you are willing to sacrifice yourself for? If not, are you at least the second slowest runner in your group? (You do have to outrun the bear. You have to outrun one person only. The bear will stop to devour the slowest runner. Or maybe it wants a snack later so you may have to outrun more than one. This is the reason I was thinking about the others on the Disney Dinosaur ride. I think my ancestors were the "grab the next biggest guy and throw him to the beasts" type. Seemed a good idea at the time.)

Just reading that paragraph gives you some idea of how slow our logical brain is. If we indeed relied upon this brain alone and we were wrong and the bear was alive and hungry, we would indeed be lunch.

So, you can see that survival would favour the fastest decision makers, but these decisions could not be made by the logical brain. It was and still is too slow. These decisions had to be made by the intuitive brain.

Also, remember this type of decision making went on for at least 30 million years and favoured those individuals who reacted properly and fastest. It is ingrained and hardwired into our system and is an integral part of our personalities. We are here because our predecessors were survivors who were the best at making the intuitive, split second decisions.

We employ these intuitive rules not just in our fight or flight decisions but in all aspects of our everyday lives. We pick up visual cues, interpret our surroundings, threats and opportunities using these "gut feel" rules and visual, auditory and pheromonic clues. It defines us and our place in the tribe and it overrules the logic center in our brain.

Here is another extreme example I found: women are found to be more attractive when they are most fertile. No kidding.

A group of students were asked to rate the attractiveness of photographs of women. They were shown photos of women wearing the same clothes and no makeup during various days of the month. The most attractive pictures were found by the students to be those of women who were ovulating. Remember, the women wore the same clothes and no makeup. How did the test subjects know? What were the visual cues?

It is also interesting to watch an individual who does not know their place in the tribe or is unable to pick up and process the subtle, non verbal clues used by the tribe. We have a name for them.

Teenagers.

And the tribal rite of passage they must pass through to learn these cues during the teenage years is grueling.

But it is not just the teenagers who tend to be poor communicators. There is one other group we have to be aware of and they tend to be highly intelligent and very well educated. In high school they excelled at chess, math and physics but rarely were considered to be the most sociable person so as a teenager they were even more handicapped. In high school they were called nerds.

So, how is all this related to investing?

Well, let's think about visual clues for a moment.

Many analysts in our industry were the chess players and math whizzes, often beyond normal intelligence levels to the point that one of my clients puts it, these folks are "wizard class" because they sell mathematics for a living.

But often these individuals are not necessarily the best communicators. And remember, in our business, part of being a good communicator is displaying a consistent message both verbally and with your body language so that the visual and auditory clues reinforce the spoken word.

What if during a market plunge the analyst employed for a big investment firm, let's call him Joe Smith, B.Comm, CGA, MBA, CFA, appears on television and says "everything will be fine . . . now is the time to buy!" but his/her body language says "I just bought a house down south based on my expected bonus this year and if the market does not recover I will have to sell it for a big loss."? What if viewers perceived that? Investors would then not hear the verbal message because their intuitive brain would override the logical message during the time of fear and, in fact, their fear would be reinforced.

Essentially this would be like being on an airplane, hearing a loud bang, and having the captain come out and tell everyone that everything is fine while his hands shake and then you notice he is wearing a parachute. We do this, but not consciously.

Here is the bottom line: Although gut feel, hardwired intuitive rules work for every other aspect of our daily life, it was never designed to deal with investing in the stock or bond markets or in mutual fund selection. In fact, this is the Great Handicap, one to which many of us are unaware that we have and it is the single greatest reason why investors, investment advisors and industry participants behave the way they do.

Remember, investing as we know it, has only been around since the stock markets were put in place in the 1800's. To a large degree, it has only really been relevant to the average individual since the late 1970's because that is when large numbers of individuals started investing on their own for the first time. Prior to that governments and big business employed most individuals and progress was measured by promotion within a bureaucracy and guaranteed pensions were part of the package. It is only when small business became the dominant job creator did individuals have to take responsibility for their own financial affairs.

Consequently, this gut feel, intuitive brain of ours interferes with the decision making necessary to invest properly.

This gut feel wakes you up half way through the night with worry, causes you to choose to listen to bad news over good news, and increases your ability to imagine the worst.

It causes us to stutter and stammer our way through the markets.

This tribal byproduct of our evolution belongs with the other vestigial appendages that we have such as our appendix and tonsils. We still need to employ it in other aspects of our lives because we are still a tribal society but we have to learn to turn off when it comes to money.

We are told to buy low and sell high but the only time we can buy low is when everyone in the tribe is worried, when the markets have fallen, when your statements are showing losses, when the tribe is selling, and your advisor's hands are shaking.

It is when the gut feel says "Run"!

How do we overcome this handicap? We have to recognize we have the handicap, get back on the ride and keep going until we conquer the fear and reach the point of wisdom.

Maybe we can watch others and learn by their mistakes. Let's see what that ride has looked like for others in the past.

Chapter 5

A Brief History of Time in the Market: How Investors and Advisors Reacted

We talked about how the only means to overcome the Great Handicap is to retrain the Gut Feel Brain. Just like my wild Disney dinosaur ride we have to do that by getting on that ride and go through it again and again.

It is hard to do this in the investment industry without putting your own money on the line and enduring about 20 years of investing experience. Of course, this will expend a considerable amount of emotional energy and you may reach a point where your worry, personal losses or level of frustration cause you to give up.

Alternatively we can begin to lay at least a foundation for you by looking through a history of the markets over an extended period of time. I propose we do this not in the traditional, boring manner of a high school history book. We are going to do this through the use of newspaper headlines and stories, and, where they are available, through brief summaries of thoughts at the time.

In the research for this book I began to have a great appreciation for diaries. I had thought that diaries were best suited for 13 year old girls who felt separate from the world and needed to write "dear diary . . ." as a way of self-soothing.

However, I discovered the value of diaries when reading about Winston Churchill, America's General George Patton and Germany's General Erwin Rommel who all wrote diaries throughout the Second World War.

These people hardly had the attitude of the average thirteen year old girl. These were leaders sending men and women to their deaths, ordering the bombing of civilians, and holding the future of not just their family, but of all the people in the country in their hands.

Here is the key point to these diaries—We know that reading history will teach us some lessons but by reading history we are automatically predisposed. That is, we know how the historical event ended (so far, anyway). Therefore, no matter how terrible things seemed back then, we know everything worked out fine. This predisposition toward a positive outcome means that history is shallower than it should be. Uncertainty adds an edge to an event, instilling a larger impact to the incident in our minds. Diaries written during the height of the uncertainty reflect that edge.

Consider how Churchill felt in August 1941 after years of war with the Nazis when every battle Britain, Canada, France, Poland, Belgium, Norway, Australia, New Zealand had fought had been lost. He was fighting the Battle of Britain. Somehow he found the courage to go on and gave his famous "We shall fight them in the fields . . ." speech.

This hindsight bias makes it seem inevitable that the Allies would win.

How did Churchill feel as the death toll of the men and women he sent into battle increased daily? What was Montgomery thinking when he faced Rommel, who had better equipment and arguably better trained soldiers? What did Nimitz think when he sent three aircraft carriers after seven Japanese carriers in an unfair fight, that on paper was doomed to failure?

These diaries are invaluable because they show what these people were thinking during the time of uncertainty when victory was not apparent and the risk to everything they held precious was at its greatest. These were the private thoughts of great men discussing their own fears, dreams and ambitions. There is much to be learned from reading this type of book.

I wish we could do the same with the history of the stock market but, unfortunately, diaries are a rare commodity in our industry.

I have had it said to me many times that "everyone knew there was a bubble in the market", whether it was about the Asian Currency Crisis and Long Term Capital's failure of 1998, the Tech Collapse of 2000 or the Market Meltdown of 2008. That was simply not true. These periods were only identified as a bubble in hindsight.

It is true that some analysts were saying that the market was going to collapse but usually the statement was made by someone who had been calling for a crash for years. We call these people "perma-bears" (to be bearish on the market is to believe it will fall and to be bullish is to believe it will rise). If you consistently say that the market will fall for a long enough period of time, eventually you will be right. Remember that even an old, broken wind up clock is right twice a day.

The fact is that most investment managers and investors never saw these bubbles coming—the thought of a bubble just was not spoken at the time.

Alright—fasten your seatbelts, make sure that your seat is in an upright and locked position and just brace yourselves. I am going to take you on quite a ride, summarized, if you can believe it, so that you go through a 20 year plus journey through the market. I am hoping that this will give you at least a hint of what investors and their advisors went through.

We will try in our review of the history of the stock markets to imbue the feeling of the times into the story. Let us begin by looking all the way back to 1981.

You will see, and let me emphasize this as strongly as I can, that the stock market is best viewed as a series of crisis interrupted by periods of relative calm.

Let's begin with March 1981 when the president of the United States, Ronald Reagan, was shot. Now, when a sitting president of the United States is shot it has a MAJOR impact on the stock market. This sent markets, that were already in crisis mode from a recession and record high interest rates, plunging, particularly with conspiracy theories abounding and the fact that we were at the height of the cold war with the Soviet Union.

In 1981 we were in a terrible recession with mortgage rates at 25% per year. Unemployment was above 10% in Canada and would go on to peak at 13% in 1982. It was equally miserable in the United States.

If you had a job you were worried about losing it. If you had a mortgage on your house at anything close to 20% you were grateful because others were paying 25%. And stock markets were down 52%. There was no place to hide.

Governments back then did what they have always done, well at least since the 1930's, cut interest rates and printed money to increase liquidity in the markets. You are going to recognize this as a recurring theme.

It took time, but eventually, like President Ronald Reagan himself, the markets recovered.

This pattern of "market crash, interest rate cuts and money injection" repeats over the years and has helped the markets to recover after every crisis. The recovery is not immediate and sometimes tries one's patience but has always come about.

The recovery of 1982/1983 was followed in 1986 by the Third World Loan crisis which took down the world banks. The countries of Mexico, Brazil, Argentina and others defaulted on the loans made to them by banks throughout the world and the banks suffered 100% losses on these loans.

Bank stock prices actually held up pretty well during the period and continued to do so right up until to August 1987.

Below are headlines from the *Globe and Mail* for that month.

Illustration 3: August 1987

AUGUST 1987

These headlines looked pretty good to investors at that time. Many investors slept comfortably thinking that their money was invested in a market where records were being broken as the market went higher and higher. We even had a good report on our federal deficit, and we had a housing boom as well as a boom in commodities, as copper, gold, nickel and zinc, all the things Canada is known for, moved higher in price.

(Actually, this sounds familiar. Have you seen these headlines more recently than 1987?)

But should you have slept well in August of 1987?

The pleasant themes of August were torn asunder soon after in one of the most violent shocks in history to stock markets throughout the world. The stock market in Canada fell 47% in three days in October 1987.

There are a number of headlines that I find fascinating. The one below from October 1987 certainly ranks as being one of the more intriguing.

This headline embodies all the aspects of fear that many associate with investing in the stock market.

<u>Illustration 4: Panic Sweeps Financial Markets</u>
<u>Smashing Records of 1929 Crash</u>

Back then stock market information was reported via ticker tape (there was no internet or all news networks) so the "enormous losses" were reported via the ticker tape reporting of stocks falling 30% to 40% in just a few hours.

Illustration 5: Panicky Investors Send Stocks Tumbling

Illustration 6: Mutual Fund Managers Try to
Stop Flood of Redemptions

Seeing these powerful headlines from more than 20 years ago still causes the hair on the back of my neck to rise. Imagine how it felt for those investors and advisors who lived through it. Fortunes were lost that day and one St.

John's advisor, who is still in the business, started his career as the market was crashing in 1987, walking into an office where the brokers were taking turns going to the bathroom to vomit.

The "flood of redemptions" discussed above is the result of investors being shocked and awed by the fall of the market. They reacted by pulling their money out of their mutual funds.

There are a large number of books discussing the 1987 crash, the feelings and expectations of the time. Panic prevailed throughout the world. An event that broke the records of the 1929 crash was not taken lightly. The thought was that we were about to go into another great depression.

In a book called *The Pension Strategy for Canadians* (Insomniac Press, 2004) author Ben Springett discusses how his parents had all their savings invested in the market during the downturn and then borrowed on their home to put more in. They sold out during the panic. Springett's book documents the personal side of the period and the tragedy that his family endured through the crash affecting the children's education fund, his parent's work life, retirement plans and the remortgaging of their house.

Another book, this time edited by Michael Lewis and properly called *Panic: The Story of Modern Financial Insanity* (W.W. Norton, 2008), is a collection of stories where one writer talks about living through the 1987 crash as an industry participant on the floor of the New York Stock Exchange. It is not a diary, unfortunately, and many of the stories are told with the benefit of hindsight. Still, one gets some sense of the abject terror, of the anguish that reduced professionals to tears and, in one rare case, accidently made one man a multimillionaire because the order system was clogged and he could not get his order in to sell his puts.

Puts are a bet against the market. They go up when the market goes down. In 1987, we were not using computers to enter orders. We were using a manual entry method. Many orders could not get filled because of the number of sell orders being entered. This gent made a bet against the market by buying a put on the market that would rise when the market fell. He had to "close" the position to lock in the profit but could not because so many trades were ahead of his. He figured the market could not fall any further and had already made a tidy profit, but he could not get the order entered. The market kept falling and by the time he did get out the market was down way below his initial sell point and he walked away with millions.

This was a rare case.

Back to my earlier point: I have had it said to me that "everyone knew there was a bubble in the market", but if that was the case then everyone should have bought puts like he did.

I urge you to pick up and read both these books.

In the book *Panic*, editor Michael Lewis goes on to discuss how legendary John Kenneth Galbraith commented on the crash.

For those who do not know of Galbraith, here is an excerpt from Wikipedia cross-referenced with his New York Times obituary:

"Galbraith was a prolific author who produced four dozen books and over a thousand articles on various subjects. Among his most famous works was a popular trilogy on economics, *American Capitalism* (1952), *The Affluent Society* (1958), and *The New Industrial State* (1967). He taught at Harvard University for many years. Galbraith was active in politics, serving in the administrations of Franklin D.

Roosevelt, Harry S. Truman, John F. Kennedy and Lyndon B. Johnson; and among other roles served as United States Ambassador to India under Kennedy."

So in 1987 when he spoke, people listened.

His comment at the time was that he was "just hoping the ensuing economic collapse wouldn't prove as painful as the Great Depression". (*Panic* page 12)

Now let's be clear here.

He wasn't questioning *if* there would be an economic collapse. That was not an issue. As one of the greatest economic minds of all time he was certain that there would be an economic collapse. He was "just hoping the ensuing economic collapse wouldn't prove as painful as the Great Depression". Can you imagine the worry at that time? No wonder Ben Springett's parents sold out. Who wouldn't?

Another commentator at the time was Faith Popcorn, a consultant who forecasts trends, or at least she tries to and has considerable credibility in such matters. After the crash of 1987 she is quoted in *Panic* as saying that the crash would cause yuppies to cut back and have "only one house, one car, one rain coat . . ."

And as for the cause for one of the worst crashes in history?

The Brady Commission was established by the US government to investigate the causes and held many expensive hearings and reviews over the following year.

It then prepared a 3000 page report summarizing the expert testimony and investigation, if a 3000 page anything can be considered a summary.

After spending all that money, taking all that time and probing into every nuance and niche, the conclusion was:

"We don't know." (*Panic* page 91)

Before we leave this, turn on one of the business news channels and note that sometime during the day the market will rise or fall just as some bit of economic news is announced. Note how the business commentator will state that the rise or fall is caused by the economic news just announced.

Very perceptive.

Consider that millions of dollars were spent by the Brady Commission over a long period of time, pulling in expert witnesses and reviewing trades and economic reports and they could not find the cause of the single greatest crash in history (to that point) but the news commentator can immediately and with total conviction tell you exactly why the market has moved in the last few minutes.

Sounds a little suspicious to me.

But let's return to 1987 for another few minutes. Fortunately, one writer for the Washington Post at the time, an economist named Robert J. Schiller, sent out a survey to professionals in the business as well as ordinary investors shortly after the 1987 crash, asking a very simple question:

"Why did you sell?"

Despite the fact that he did not spend millions of tax payer's money calling in experts and holding public hearings, he did manage to reach a conclusion.

The most important reason that survey participants said they sold was that they heard that the stock market was falling. (*Panic* page 68)

So, let's consider that point for a moment—the primary reason that one of the greatest crashes in history occurred, one that supposedly presaged the collapse of the Western economic system, was because investors, both the pros and your average Joe's, heard that the market was falling.

This is a classic case of the market falling because of herd movement.

Further evidence that the market crash was caused by nothing more than herd movement was that the economy did not collapse. Even Galbraith was surprised.

In fact, in economic terms, nothing happened. Nothing at all.

The prevailing sense of gloom and doom continued for some time but gradually the shock wore off and people realized that the end of the world was not nigh. Things started to turn for the better.

Mind you, in response to the market fall, interest rates were cut and money was injected by various central banks around the world. There is the recurring theme. Cutting interest rates and printing money are an economic stimulus because it does two things. Cutting interest rates makes stocks more valuable and lowers the cost of borrowing.

Think about this—why do people invest in stocks?

People invest in stocks because they believe stocks will deliver them more money in the future than if they kept the money in their savings account. One of the biggest costs to any company is the cost of borrowing money. If you lower that cost you increase the probability of a company making more money in the future so if you cut the cost of borrowing you increase the chances that a listed public company (a stock) will rise in value. Also lowering the interest rate makes it less beneficial to keep money in the bank so stocks look like a better choice.

Printing money makes more money available for borrowing. Yes, the government literally creates money by loaning cash in large quantities at a low interest rate to the banks and related institutions. Then the banks have reserves of cash that they can then loan out to consumers. Mortgage rates, car loan rates and business loan rates are brought down and "cheap money" is readily available.

Such easy credit means that people can afford a newer, larger house, new appliances and new cars and, despite the sense of depression, people start to buy and businesses start to expand.

For the economy this is like tromping on the gas pedal in your car.

The cash injection was made as the market was crashing and it took time for the lower interest rates and plentiful amounts of money to have their effect on the system.

The market stabilized in late 1987 and in 1988 the yuppies went on a buying binge. In fact, it only took to June of 1989, 18 months after the crash, for the markets to reach their old record highs of August 1987. Surprised?

The governments then chose to take their foot off the gas and actually apply the brakes by increasing interest rates to slow down the booming economy.

Those who sold in the panic of October 1987 lost. Those who held on recovered everything.

Now let's turn to the headlines of June 1990 when the markets had fully recovered all the previous losses. These headlines are a sharp contrast to those of October of 1987.

Illustration 7: Economy Grows in March Despite High Interest Rates

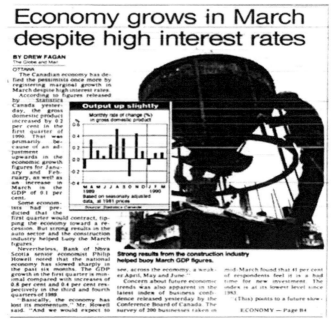

Illustration 8: Optimism on Earnings,
Rates Boosts Markets

It is hard to believe that such an incredibly positive change could occur in such a short period of time, particularly given such extreme predictions of disaster in October 1987.

Understand that the economy was then so strong that the government had to do the opposite of what it did in 1987. Now it had to raise rates and reduce the money supply. That is quite a turnaround.

This good news kept coming as reported by the *Wall Street Journal* discussing the second quarter profits of 1990 in the headline below:

Illustration 9: Positives Aplenty Seen in Quarter's Profits

Positives Aplenty Seen in Quarter's Profits

By DOUGLAS R. SEASE
And CHRISTOPHER WINANS

Staff Reporters of THE WALL STREET JOURNAL

NEW YORK—Despite scattered earnings disappointments, such as the announcements earlier this week by American Telephone & Telegraph Co. and Caterpillar Inc., the overall outlook for second-quarter profits holds more hope than horror.

AT&T and Caterpillar shocked investors by disclosing that earnings aren't meeting expectations. AT&T said Wednesday that its second-quarter profit probably will be below year-earlier results, while Caterpillar said Monday that it expects current-year earnings will be "substantially lower" than last year's.

But analysts and money managers say there is little evidence of earnings problems at many other large companies. Indeed, they are counting on seeing plenty of pleasant surprises in coming weeks, as

corporations report their second-quarter results.

This is good news for investors who have a broadly diversified portfolio of stocks. The flood of second-quarter earnings reports to be released in the next few weeks isn't likely to wash the value of these investors' shares down the drain.

At the same time, however, investors who are heavily committed to a single stock that dares to disappoint Wall Street with worse-than-expected results had better brace themselves. They're apt to get hammered.

That's the lesson analysts and money managers find in the seemingly paradoxical performance of the Dow Jones Industrial Average and AT&T, a key component of the industrial average, following Wednesday's announcement. That day, irritated investors dumped AT&T shares, driving the price down $2.125, to $39.125, on volume of 11.5 million shares. AT&T's

Please Turn to Page C10, Column 6

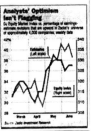

Analysts' Optimism Isn't Flagging

Dow Jones Industrial Average

Ruling Draws the Worried to 'Living Wills'

And you have heard of the "Roaring Twenties"? This referenced the 1920's when the North American economies boomed like never before.

Illustration 10: New Mirror, Old Image: the 1920's Again?

New Mirror, Old Image: the 1920s Again?

In 15-Year Pattern, '90 Aligns With '29

HEARD ON THE STREET

By Roger Lowenstein
Staff Reporter of THE WALL STREET JOURNAL

NEW YORK—Michael Belkin, a Salomon Brothers analyst, looks at the historical record of the stock market and finds it disconcerting.

Only twice in this century has the Dow Jones Industrial Average risen in five consecutive years. The first was in the roaring Twenties, 1924-1928; the other was the past five years, 1985-1989.

Comparing the 1980s with the past decade isn't new, but Mr. Belkin's study adds a twist. "Most people who have thought about this have wondered whether 1987—the year of the modern stock market crash—corresponded to 1929," he says. If so, that's largely the period the fear that a latter-day version of the 1930s Depression lurks around the corner.

But looking at history, a different kind of pattern emerges, Mr. Belkin says. Specifically, he evenly aligns years since 1974, the stock market has moved the same direction—falling or rising—as it did 61 years earlier.

Coincidence? Perhaps. But Mr. Belkin is in part a technical analyst, and technical analysts pay a lot of attention to past market patterns. And he says that 1989—the year of the Great Crash—bears more resemblance to the current year, 1990, than to 1987. Stock prices also were rising for a while in 1929, but they ended the year down 17%. They fell further in 1930 and dropped more sharply still in 1931.

Although Mr. Belkin doesn't actually expect another Depression, his conclusion

may be stated simply: "It's late in the market cycle and not the time for wild-eyed speculation."

Fundamental investors may view as wild-eyed any attempt to predict stock prices on the basis of what happened 61 years earlier. But Mr. Belkin's study is noteworthy not so much because it repeats themselves in lockstep, but because the behavior of people who participate in markets does tend to recur.

The real point of Mr. Belkin's exercise, he says, is that for "very much believes in economic cycles and in market cycles. Bull markets don't last forever; at least, the bull markets in gold, oil, real estate, technology stocks, junk bonds, Japanese equities and Donald Trump didn't last forever.

Why is that relevant? "It's late in the market cycle and the time for wild-eyed speculation, I'm going to be looking for the stock market rally, it can be argued that people have been buying because the market has been buying for different reasons.

People are buying because the market is going up. That's exactly what's going on," he says. And Mr. Belkin, head of research at Salomon Street, all the acquisition-crazed money managers will tell you that's true of the small investor but that they're buying for different reasons. But the truth

is, it's the same. They don't want to miss the rise.

This is worth pondering. If markets fell in 1929 (and for three years thereafter) after a five-year bull market in the '20s, why does the five-year bull market of the late 1980s guarantee that markets will rise in 1990?

It doesn't. Yet investors small and large are pouring money into stocks, largely because they have been watching the market rise.

James Solloway, chief economist of Argus Research, disputes this view. He says there is "something fundamental" spurring the rise. "It's more than the herd instinct," he says. "The fact is, we have had a sharp decline in interest rates and a shift in perceptions" regarding the economy.

Nonetheless, he concedes that the herd instinct "does help to build a momentum." And, noting that cash levels of mutual funds managers have reached a record low, he adds: "There is a certain amount of pressure on money managers. Like the lottery, you gotta be in it to win it."

In Mr. McAllister's view, the various reasons offered for the market's rise are just rationalizations. But "there's have a

Please Turn to Page C8, Column 3

47

So, we went from extreme depression, almost literally, to extreme optimism, all within 24 months. What was an investor to think? How could the sages of the market be so wrong in October of 1987, including the great Galbraith? Terms like "palpable fear", so common such a short time ago, were forgotten. The yuppies certainly did not "cocoon" as Faith Popcorn had thought. They were buying more in 1990 than they had in 1987.

And projections that profits in the future would be even better? Wow!

But all was not to be as rosy as expected. The headlines of June 1990 were followed by another severe downturn bringing the market down again in October 1990 to the October 1987 lows.

This fall was triggered by several events.

In August of 1990, Iraq invaded Kuwait and the United Nations coalition put together forces in preparation for war. By the time that October 1990 rolled around the markets had fallen dramatically, investors were selling out, and the headlines below captured the feelings of the time.

Illustration 11: Money Managers Learn Humility
Amid the Bull Market's Ashes

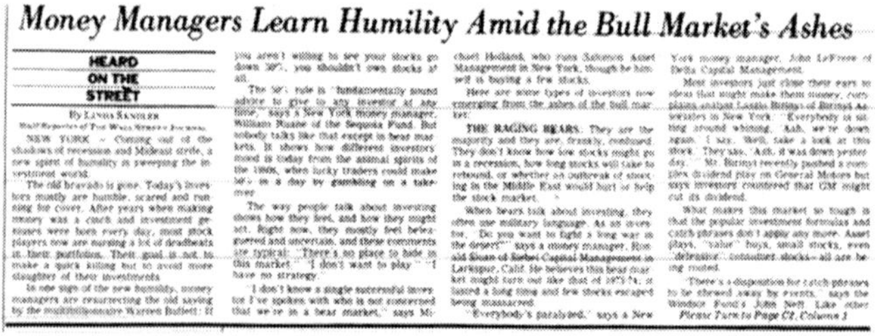

Within the article it discusses how investors "did not want to play" and how "no strategies were working". Once again, everything fell and there was no end in sight but the wallowing misery of all the fear that a long war in the desert would bring.

Bear in mind that in October 1990 the United Nations Coalition was openly discussing going to war with Saddam Hussein who had already used chemical weapons on his own people. Iraq had the third largest standing army in the world, and was pledging to provide the mother of all battles. The prospects were for a long and costly war and the possibility of oil prices skyrocketing were extremely high.

At the same time, we were going through another recession with worries about government deficits and the cost of the war adding to these worries. The unemployment rate was again above 10% and one year interest rates were costing home owners 14%+ on their mortgages. It was not as severe as 1980 but it felt like it and for many first time home buyers and those just entering the workforce, it was miserable.

This was the first full blown economic crisis in my career. I was two years in this business then and the company I was working for still operated on the "idea of the week", the idea being the stock we were going to recommend that week to create transactions and therefore commissions. It was safe to say that we were out of ideas.

We were called stockbrokers back then and tax reduction strategies, estate and succession planning and overall financial planning rarely, if ever, was discussed.

It was a rough time. I remember wondering if I would ever survive in this career. The headlines of 1990 in Canada were pretty dismal as noted below.

Illustration 12: October 1990

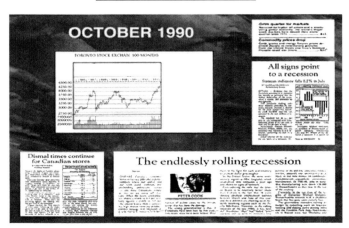

These are from the *Globe and Mail* and talk about how terrible the economy was, it seemed like we were in an endless recession.

Mind you, in response to the market fall, interest rates were cut and money was injected by various central banks around the world.

We got through October 1990 but the misery continued through to January 1991. The UN Coalition had built up its armed forces and the world held its breath for the mother of all battles. Saddam Hussein kept launching chemical rockets and one wondered when he would launch a nuclear armed missile. Times were tense. During those months there were public discussions from big names in the investment business such as Fidelity, Smith Barney, Merrill Lynch and others about how far the market would fall once UN Coalition finally attacked.

"On January 17, 1991, at 3 A.M. Baghdad time, ten U.S. F-117 Nighthawk stealth bombers under the protection of a three-ship formation of EF-111s bombed Baghdad, the capital of Iraq. The force came under fire from 3,000 anti-aircraft guns firing from rooftops in Baghdad." (Source *Wikipedia*)

I remember this distinctly. I was working late at the office and CNN was in its infancy. We had a very primitive intranet in the company. A flash went across my computer monitor saying Baghdad was being bombed, oil prices spiked to over $40 per barrel from about $26 in the next few minutes, and I decided to go home and prepare my resume to look for another job. I knew from the experts that the market was going to fall even further tomorrow and my clients' money and my career were toast.

But the next day the market opened up some 500 points, which was considered an unheard of, massive gain at the time. Fidelity later admitted that it could not wait for the market to fall as everyone expected and figured they would buy at the open, surprising everyone and trumping their competition. The market surged higher and restored investors' confidence, at least to some degree.

But it was not just the war with Iraq that we were worried about. We had a housing collapse and banking crisis in the US as well at the same time.

It is a bit ironic that from 1990 through to 1992 we had a US president named Bush, a war in Iraq and a US banking crisis and in 2008 we had a US president named Bush, a war in Iraq and a US banking crisis. Who says that history does not repeat itself?

The banking crisis in 1990 to 1992 involved smaller banks but there were a lot of them. All tolled 1,047 "Thrifts" or smaller local banks in the US failed. Once again the culprit was the mortgage market. Homeowners defaulted on their mortgages, homes were foreclosed on and real estate prices fell. The total cost to the American tax payer was estimated to be $153 billion which is about $255 billion in 2008 dollars.

The apparatus that was set up back then to address the problem was Resolution Trust Corporation, an arm of the US government set up specifically to take over the failing banks. We also had our problems in Canada with real estate as well including the bankruptcy of some high profile projects including Canary Wharf (The Reichmann Brothers) and West Edmonton Mall (The Germazians).

From the bottom of the market in October 1990 until early 1992 the market was up about 25%. But in December 1992 and January 1993 the newspaper headlines from the *Globe and Mail* were still pretty depressing.

<u>Illustration 13: Dec. 1992 / Jan. 1993</u>

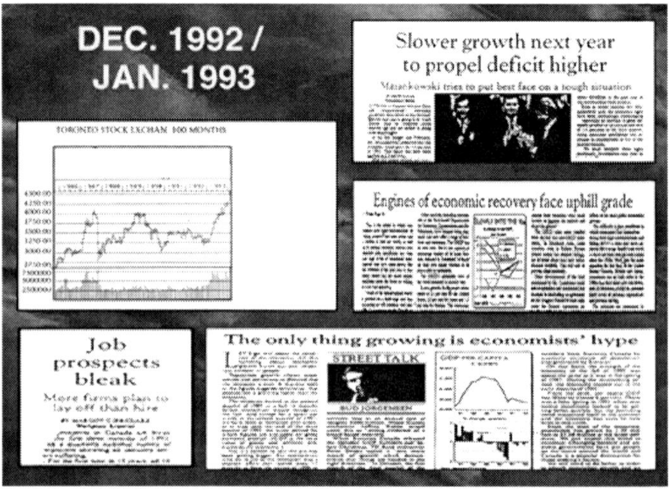

By the end of 1993, the Toronto Stock Exchange levels surged 43% and finally broke into new all time highs.

And then the next calamity arose.

The Charlottetown Accord was an attempt to unite Canada in 1993 and instead ended up as a fiasco.

It was defeated when the Premier of Newfoundland and Labrador and one single MP in the House of Commons objected. Again there was uncertainty and turmoil in the market and there were forecasts that the markets were going to crash if these agreements were not approved. Ironically, the markets fell before the agreement was voted on and rose after the defeat was announced.

It was during 1993 that we had a major event occur in Newfoundland and Labrador, one that keeps us all glued to the junior mining sector. It was during this time that I had a call from Peter Dimmell, one of the most brilliant geologists I have ever met. He told me of a discovery called Voisey's Bay in Labrador. He told me to go talk to the discoverers.

Then another client, who was also a geologist, came to see me with what looked like the expression that one would expect if they had seen the dead come back to life. He had seen the actual drill core from the Voisey's Bay discovery (that had been referenced in their most recent press release) and said it was the most incredible core ever found on the planet.

I called the mining analyst of the firm I was working with at the time and had my client describe the drill core to him. I was working with a big, national firm and the analyst was a "big" analyst. He said that he had read the press release and believed that it was not credible. He said that no drill core could be that rich and instead of recommending that I buy the stock he immediately put a sell recommendation on it on behalf of the firm which meant no advisor in the firm, including me could recommend it for any client.

Let me put this in context. Peter Dimmell had made the single best recommendation of his life. He had recommended a stock at pennies per share that was eventually sold for, all things adjusted, $250 PER SHARE. It was painful to sit on the sidelines and watch this happen and not be able to participate.

The discoverers, Verbiski and Chislett, took it all when they properly set up the Voisey's Bay discovery and turned the province of Newfoundland and Labrador into the Saudi Arabia of nickel by finding 25% of all the nickel on the planet.

This brings us to 1994 when one of the largest insurance companies in Canada, Confederation Life, went bankrupt. This was a big, established, "blue chip" (meaning very reliable and stable company) that turned turtle in a surprisingly quick manner.

And to add to the worry, in December of 1994 the Mexican Currency crisis hit and knocked down the markets further. The crises arose when the Mexican government unexpectedly announced a devaluation of its currency.

This shock had further reverberations. At the time, Canada was facing mounting federal government deficits as were most of the provinces, our economic outlook was poor and unemployment high. Our Canadian dollar was starting to fall precipitously against the American currency. At this point in time, the *Wall Street Journal* was calling Canada a third world country and our dollar was "the peso of the North".

Shortly after that we had the Quebec Referendum. On October 30, 1995, 50.58% of the voters in Quebec chose to stay in Canada. Talk about winning by a whisker.

All of these crises were serious and created great tribulation at the time. In fact, looking at this litany, you can understand my earlier point that the stock market is really a series of calamities interrupted by brief periods of calm. We survived each of these trials but these were big worries at the time and caused investors to sell out to move to "safer" short term investments.

But, despite all this flotsam and jetsam, the markets went on to new highs and new challenges. The calm was then broken once again in 1997 when the largest scandal to ever hit the Toronto Stock Exchange arose when the stock of mining giant Bre-X collapsed.

On a personal level, we had 22 clients in Bre-X, one of which was very new and she had found the Bre-X share certificate on her father's desk after he had become senile. It was worth, at the time, just over $1 million. Her father had put in about $50,000 so the gain was $950,000 to that point. She had come to me because she had heard I had some expertise in tax reduction strategies and she asked how I could lower the tax on such a gain.

There are eight ways to Tuesday to lower taxes but the first rule of investing is to not lose the gain at all. Shortly after we had met, our mining analyst sent a note about how a company called Freeport McMoran had been "given" the right to buy Bre-X by the very corrupt President of the Philippines, Ferdinand Marcos. The analyst noted that "if we wanted to participate in the upside with less risk we should sell Bre-X and buy Freeport" and he really meant it. This was once when the judgment of the analyst was spot on.

We made this recommendation to our clients and 20 out of the 22 clients sold Bre-X and bought Freeport. Shortly thereafter Freeport said it had inspected the Bre-X property and could find no gold. Then we heard that the chief geologist of Bre-X had jumped out of a helicopter in an apparent suicide.

Bre-X was a company that had fooled everyone into believing it had a massive gold discovery, including Freeport, when in fact it had no gold at all. Freeport announced that it was not going to buy Bre-X and the stock went into a death spiral as every investor tried to sell at the same time.

Unfortunately, my $1 million client had asked another firm for a second opinion and stayed in. They did not lose any money, depending on your perspective—they got about $50,000 back.

The size and extent of the fraud was amazing and effectively put the credibility of the Toronto Stock Exchange into question and put the entire mining sector under suspicion. Remember, the Toronto Stock Exchange is the top place in the world to raise money for mining ventures. The impact of the Bre-X scandal was disastrous.

Around this time I also met with another new client who provided me with another great lesson. Her husband had died and he had handled all the money in the family for years. He knew that there was something called a kitchen but never ventured into it and she knew nothing about money. We see this often with older clients where there was a division of responsibility based on the number of Y chromosomes, and still see it to some extent today, which is a real shame because more often than not, the wife becomes the ultimate decision maker for the family's legacy.

Remember, women are statistically more often the ultimate deciders of where the family's wealth will be distributed. They live longer than men. Yet women are generally less financially literate than their husbands.

This lady, and I use that word in the truest of its meaning, was in her early 70's and fortunately one of the smartest people I have ever met and one who I was always fondest of.

True to form, she did not know anything about investing even though she was left a fortune. She did not know even know how to write a cheque

That changed fast. Within a few months she was writing cheques and was asking some of the most basic and keenest questions I had ever heard. If this woman had been only a few years younger I probably would have hired her and given her my money to manage.

At one point in early 1998, she called and said "I figured out that last year you earned me 44% and I have called three friends and told them to come see you because they want to earn 44% too." I pointed out that she was the one that had suggested that she would be happy with Canadian bank stocks and that was the reason her account had increased. Further, it was impossible for me to promise a 44% increase for her or her friends next year.

Again, with time, the Toronto market recovered from the Confederation Life bankruptcy, the Quebec Referendum crises and the Bre-X Scandal and began to reach all time highs in 1998 as indicated by the March 7, 1998 headline from the *Globe and Mail* below.

Illustration 14: TSE Flirts With the Record Zone

Sure enough, by March 10, 1998 we had these two headlines:

Illustration 15: TSE 300 Reclaims Record High

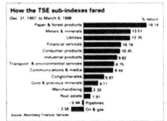

Illustration 16: TSE 300 Index Continues Record Ways

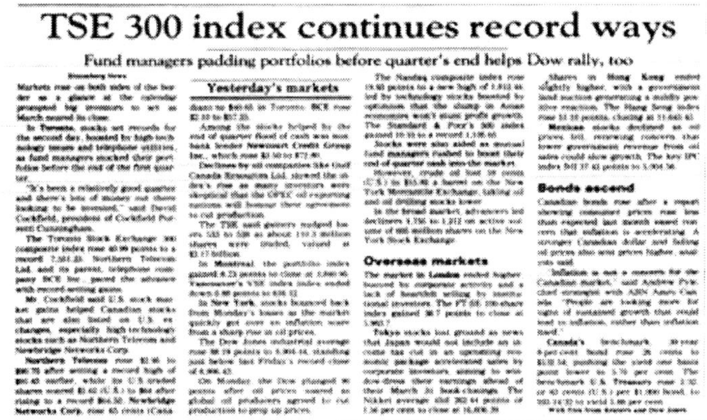

TSE 300 index continues record ways

Fund managers padding portfolios before quarter's end helps Dow rally, too

Yesterday's markets

Overseas markets

Bonds ascend

And as the headline below shows, with markets going to new highs, this prompted more investors to put more money ito the markets. In fact by March 17, 1998 more Canadians had more money in mutual funds than any other time in history.

Illustration 17: Fund Assets Soar to Record

Fund assets soar to record

Reach $305.2-billion, boosted by surging global stock markets, sales during RRSP season

How mutual funds have fared in February

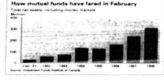

I have to stop you here. I want to take this opportunity to clear up a few most commonly misunderstood terms in our industry: Mutual Funds and RRSP's.

We have, over the years, met some incredible people with large amounts of money. A lot of them have no idea what they are invested in. Do not be embarrassed if you are the same. Let me give you an example of such a situation.

A new client comes to see us. Has a great education and at least 20 years of investing. He says "I hate the stock market. I am only invested in mutual funds." Turns out he is ONLY invested in mutual funds that are 100% exposed to the stock market. He does not know this.

Similar story: One of my partners in our practice overhears a conversation between two women at the local shopping mall. One lady says: "My investments fell and I have lost a lot of money." Her friend says "You should buy an RRSP. They do great."

Understand that an RRSP is a type of an investment account, like a bucket. You put money in the bucket. The RRSP manager can invest that bucket of money anywhere that is specified in the RRSP agreement, INCLUDING THE STOCK MARKET.

So, you can have an RRSP invested in stocks, bonds, mutual funds, Guaranteed Investement Certificates, etc. The RRSP itself is not an investment. The underlying investment is good or bad depending on what you invest in.

The same logic holds true for Tax Free Savings Accounts.

Please understand that there is no shame is asking basic questions about what your money is invested in. We spend a lot of time on client investment literacy (please note said book). It is not because we are being altruistic. It is because a knowledgeable client makes more money than a client who does not understand what they are investing in, and if our clients make more money, we do too. We are not trying to turn our clients, or you, into investment advisors, but we are trying to turn our clients, and you, into knowledgeable consumers.

So, to be clear: **THERE IS NO SUCH THING AS A DUMB QUESTION IN OUR BUSINESS!**

There are dumb answers but this is about money. If your advisor intimidates you or makes you feel stupid for asking questions, fire him/her. Their job is to explain. If they haven't explained your investments to you in a way that makes you feel comfortable, they have failed in doing their job. I really cannot emphasize this enough. Most dissappointment and outright frauds have arisen when an advisor cannot answer these basic questions—where is my money invested and how does it make money?

Lets go back to 1998 when we had talk of mergers among the six largest Canadian banks, which pushed their stock prices to all time highs, and we also saw the first snippets of high growth from BCE and Nortel.

The optimism was also was seen across the border in the US as shown by these headlines from the *Wall Street Journal*.

Illustration 18: Plunging Oil Prices Catapult Stocks to Records

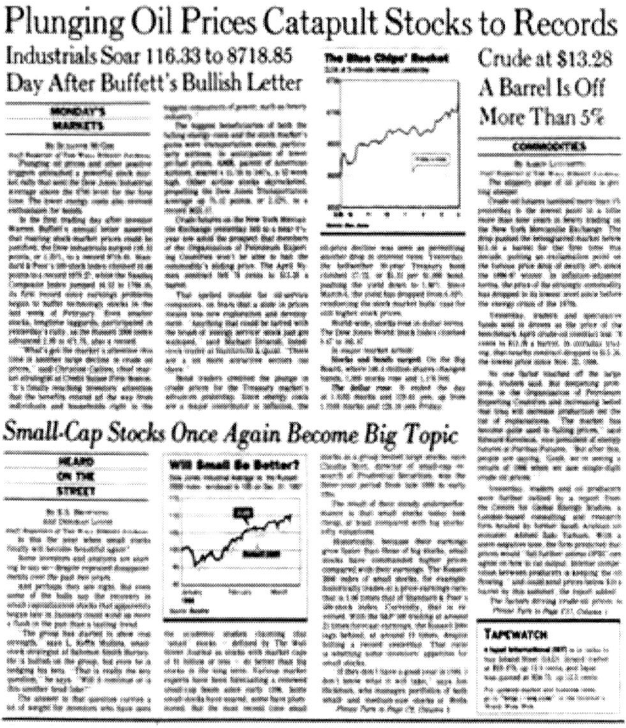

Plunging Oil Prices Catapult Stocks to Records

Industrials Soar 116.33 to 8718.85 Day After Buffett's Bullish Letter

Crude at $13.28 A Barrel Is Off More Than 5%

Small-Cap Stocks Once Again Become Big Topic

On March 21, 1998 the US market broke all time highs again.

Illustration 19: Dow Smashes 8,900-Point Barrier

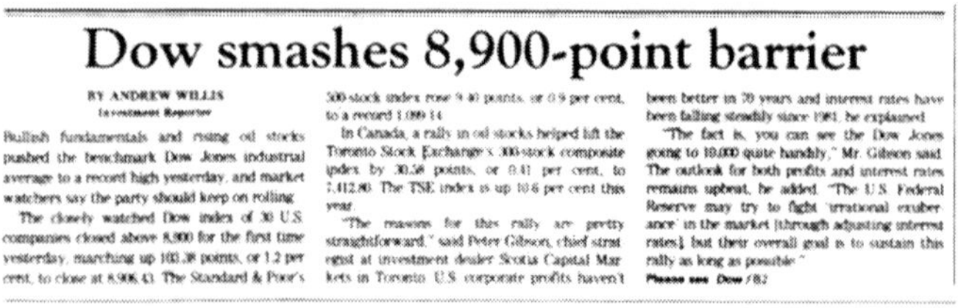

Dow smashes 8,900-point barrier

BY ANDREW WILLIS
Investment Reporter

Bullish fundamentals and rising oil stocks pushed the benchmark Dow Jones industrial average to a record high yesterday, and market watchers say the party should keep on rolling.

The closely watched Dow index of 30 U.S. companies closed above 8,900 for the first time yesterday, marching up 103.38 points, or 1.2 per cent, to close at 8,906.43. The Standard & Poor's 500-stock index rose 9.40 points, or 0.9 per cent, to a record 1,099.14.

In Canada, a rally in oil stocks helped lift the Toronto Stock Exchange's 300-stock composite index by 30.58 points, or 0.41 per cent, to 7,412.80. The TSE index is up 10.6 per cent this year.

"The reasons for this rally are pretty straightforward," said Peter Gibson, chief strategist at investment dealer Scotia Capital Markets in Toronto. U.S. corporate profits haven't been better in 20 years and interest rates have been falling steadily since 1981, he explained.

"The fact is, you can see the Dow Jones going to 10,000 quite handily," Mr. Gibson said. The outlook for both profits and interest rates remains upbeat, he added. "The U.S. Federal Reserve may try to fight 'irrational exuberance' in the market [through adjusting interest rates], but their overall goal is to sustain this rally as long as possible."

Please see Dow / B2

So, by now, you can suspect what happened next. This wondrous time and optimism peaked in March of 1998 and ended rather quickly with the following headline on September 1, 1998 from the *Globe and Mail*.

<u>Illustration 20: Investors Flee Markets</u>

In the summer of 1998 the Asian Currency Crises and Long Term Capital crisis had hit, contributing to Russia going bankrupt in August of 1998.

By September 1998 most of the Canadian banks were off by more than 30% from their peak with one bank down 60% from its all time high six months previously.

The September 5, 1998 headline below is from the *London Times* (yes, of England).

Illustration 21: Investors Run For Cover

Investors run for cover

Panic share selling has erupted across global markets. **Caroline Merrell** examines the investment options

And this one is from the *Wall Street Journal* on the same day.

Illustration 22: Investors' Dreams Fade Further Away

Quarterly Review • Third Quarter 2002

STOCK MARKET

THE WALL STREET JOURNAL

Investors' Dreams Fade Further Away

Even Optimists Brace For 3rd Straight Year Of Market Declines

And the depressing headlines just kept coming. Here is the *Wall Street Journal* on September 11, 1998.

Illustration 23: Dow Industrials Plunge 249.48, or 3.17%

The seriousness of the time was perhaps best evidenced by Michael Lewis' article in the New York Times, January 24, 1999 as told in his book *Panic* (page 133).

Lewis quotes Robert Rubin, the then Secretary of the Treasury in the US, as stating "the world is experiencing the worst financial crisis in 50 years". Rubin had worked and lived through the 1987 crash, only 11 years before. So, according to no less than the Secretary of the Treasury of the United States of America himself, the 1998 crash was even worse than the 1987 crash.

And, adding to the voices of concern was Alan Greenspan. He was Chairman of the Federal Reserve at the time and, again according to Lewis, he "had never seen anything in his lifetime that compared to the terror of August of 1998".

In the face of these statements the headlines then become better understood. We had just been warming up to the idea that Asia was to be the growth region for the next century and here we had the Asian economies in shambles.

As well with Russia bankrupt it was thought for certain the world economy was due to contract even further. And Long Term Capital, a hedge fund run by two Nobel Prize winning economists, had contributed to the catastrophe by amassing such a large losing position that it had to be bailed out by Wall Street banks after the intervention of the U.S. government. Had it been allowed to collapse, the downturn would have been much worse.

Therefore, when the author of the newspaper article below wrote that "most agree that the bull market that has enriched ordinary investors and moved fund managers into high rent districts isn't going to reappear any time soon" you can appreciate where he was coming from.

<u>Illustration 24: Investors Flee Markets</u>

I want to examine that headline a little more closely.

To begin with, I have always had trouble with the way that economic information is reported as being current. That is, this headline is posted on September 1 reporting on what happened on the last day of August 1998 but it is written in current tense.

The headline reads "Investors FLEE the markets . . ." when in fact investors FLED the markets because it happened yesterday.

Similarly, "Panic . . . drives Dow down 6 percent, spills . . ." is suggesting that this is happening now. Should that not be "Panic . . . DROVE Dow down 6%, SPILLED . . ."?

Finally, "Investors switch to cash" should be "Investors SWITCHED to cash."

This may seem trivial but it is hard enough keeping investors from pulling out without the addition of present tense suggesting that the panic continues. The panic may have continued, partly because of these headlines, but that would not be reported until the next day.

So, by now you know the story.

Mind you, in response to the market fall, interest rates were cut and money was injected by various central banks around the world.

And once again, the resiliency of the markets proved the experts wrong and it only took 18 months for the market to recover.

In fact, the markets more than just recovered—they rose 109% from September 1998 to the peak of the market in 2000. So much for "Russia Bear Kills US Bull For Good" and ". . . experts agree on one thing . . . that the market won't recover any time soon.".

No sooner were we breaking all time highs than a new worry emerged. In fairness, it had been talked about for a long time but was coming to a head during 1999. This was, of course, the Y2K problem that would stop elevators elevating, airplanes flying, and nuclear power plants humming at 12:01 a.m. January 1, 2000.

So serious was this issue that the state owned airline of China ordered all its engineers that were charged with solving the Y2K problem on the airplane computers to be in the air on these very planes on New Year's Eve, 1999. Talk about job performance pressure.

However, Y2K became Y2 nothing and within a few months the markets reached a new peak in May of 2000. This time it was the high tech stocks that reached the peak of their bubble.

Below is the *Globe and Mail* on March 2, 2000.

<u>Illustration 25: Reports Show U.S. Economy Sizzling</u>

And here is the *Wall Street Journal* on March 10, 2000.

<u>Illustration 26: Nasdaq Pumps Up to 5000</u>

Copyright Wall Street Journal. All rights reserved.

This is from the *Globe and Mail* on March 19, 2000.

Illustration 27: Funds Hitch Onto High-Tech Rocket Ride

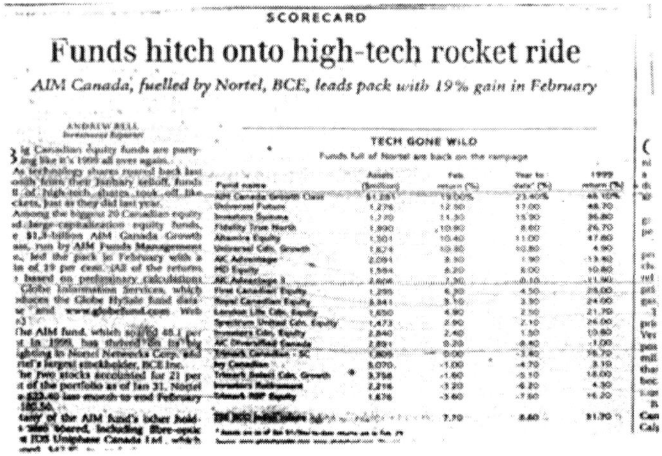
SCORECARD

Funds hitch onto high-tech rocket ride

AIM Canada, fuelled by Nortel, BCE, leads pack with 19% gain in February

TECH GONE WILD

And of course investors were attracted to these funds and were calling their advisors and asking to invest in them and the mutual fund salespeople saw an easy sell.

These funds had returned phenomenal results the previous year with the top performers returning 48% in 1999 and 23% up to the end of February in 2000. So, how could you lose? I mean even if the fund only returned half that this year I think that is pretty good.

See, the perception is often that a fund that has been rising has some sort of momentum so that even if it slows down you will make some money. Unfortunately, this is not true. There are only two directions for a fund—either forward or back and the direction can change at a moment's notice. The speed of the fund depends on the underlying investments and the technical term in the industry is "Beta".

So, technology funds have high betas, meaning they move up and down quite quickly compared to other funds.

And, of course, the fine print noting that "past performance does not indicate future performance . . ." was read but that is in every ad, even the losing ones, right?

Optimism abounded as a new age of prosperity and a new era of economics was heralded. This was the time when startup dotcom companies could burn through millions of dollars of investors' money with no hope of profit and still have their shares rise to astronomically high values.

And it was not just the average Joe's who were caught up in the mania. Many established firms including Cisco Systems and Yahoo bought startups at incredibly high prices but with headlines like those above you can see how the media was caught up with the mania.

So, in the spirit of the high tech swoon, companies that had no earnings or even any hope of earnings were being listed as startups and rising to astounding highs. I remember one listing of an internet bank that gave every new account $5 to open an account. What do you think happened there? It rose dramatically when it was first listed but shortly after ran out of money. Can't imagine why.

One of my favorite articles is the one below from the *Globe and Mail* in June 2000 asking ". . . how much good news can an investor stand?".

It states that if Bell Canada and Nortel were not included in the Toronto Stock Exchange then the entire exchange would have only risen about 2% from the previous year. This was true.

In fact the Canadian banks had hardly recovered from their lows reached in 1998 and with oil at $10 per barrel and gold at $268 an ounce, the other sectors of the Canadian market place had fallen. The argument was that there were a lot more potential gains left in the market.

<u>Illustration 28: Everything's Coming Up Roses,
Analysts Say</u>

Also, the analysts quoted in here include a pretty good listing of firms such as those of bank owned firms in Canada and Goldman Sachs in the US. These analysts were all forecasting that the markets would continue to rise in 2000, just not as much as they had risen in 1999.

So, if the big guys were forecasting that we were going higher and their logic seemed sound, the economy was booming, and fund manager returns were terrific, what was an investor to do?

You know what happened next.

The markets peaked between March and August of 2000 and began a disastrous decline. Nortel, which had grown to be approximately 30% of the entire Toronto Stock Exchange index began a sharp and precipitous fall throughout the remainder of 2000 and into 2001.

There was much debate and discussion as to the cause of the market decline and probably the best explanation was offered by Mr. Lloyd Williams, a former investment advisor who now serves as one of the top coaches in the industry. (Yes, advisors have coaches.)

His research pointed, ironically, to the Y2K problem. We did get bitten by it, but in an unexpected manner.

He suggests that in a "normal" business cycle large businesses and governments would replace one third of their computers in any one year. In this way, one third of the employees would have new computers, one third would have one year old computers and the remaining employees would only have to tolerate their old computer for one more year. The same goes for routers, software and related services and products. This meant that a regular amount of money could be budgeted annually for computer upgrading, and within large bureaucracies, regularity is a good thing.

Y2K disrupted this pattern and forced companies to purchase three year's worth of computer equipment, technology and services in one year—1999. This increased level of technology also enabled more applications to be used driving demand and opening up the emerging internet arena just as the dotcom concept began to arise. Consequently, the increased demand that the technology manufacturers, both software and hardware, were seeing was thought to be a new, higher and sustainable level of business and the industry ramped up for it, but the level was not sustainable. It was a one-off.

In addition to Lloyd Williams thoughts consider that Allan Greenspan, chair of the Fed in the US, raised interest rates six times during 1999 and 2000 on the belief that all the growth happening in the economy spurred on by the high tech purchases would lead to inflation and other governments, including Canada's, raised interest rates as well. This was done to slow the economy.

The turn came quickly.

I distinctly remember a conference call about Intel in April of 2000 because it was such an odd call. Technology companies are considered "growth" companies because they grow faster than the economy and high tech firms like Intel during this time were growing at incredible rates because they had three years of orders packed into one year. This was used to justify their high share prices.

In contrast, "value" companies are firms that have hard assets such as bricks and mortar, minerals, and oil. Value companies tend to be banks (real ones, not fairytale internet versions), insurance, mining, oil and manufacturing companies. They are valued in the same way as you would appraise your house. You determine the replacement value of the company's assets, how much cash did the company have and how hard was it for a rival to enter into their business. These were key questions. If the company was selling for less than appraised value, it was undervalued.

In the year 2000 value stocks were deplored because all the underlying holdings had fallen in value (oil down from $18 to $10 per barrel, gold had fallen from $450 an ounce to $268 an ounce and the Canadian banks were still at the levels of September 1998) while the growth stocks (high tech) had soared.

As reported in April 2000, for the March 2000 quarter end Intel's sales revenue had dropped dramatically but the analyst had noted that the company had so much cash on hand it had little to worry about.

I remember thinking this odd that a measure normally used for a value company (cash) was being used to suggest that shares of a growth company should rise, particularly when its sales, the single most important measure for growth companies, had fallen.

In hindsight, there were more clues.

No inflation arose largely because the cost of oil and materials fell during the period. The effect of the interest rate rise was to put the brakes on to slow the economy and when the technology buying stopped, which was the real reason that the economy had been growing anyway, you had a double whammy and the economy effectively stopped. Down came the markets.

The markets continued to fall throughout 2000 into 2001 and there was a start of an initial recovery during early 2001. It was thought that maybe the worst was over and we were about to resume growth.

The morning of September 11, 2001 changed all that when the attack took place on the World Trade Center, 3000 people died, and the markets tumbled.

We have had many headlines during the 2008 market crash proclaiming that various days were "the worst day in the history of the market".

They weren't.

Nothing can compare to seeing live TV coverage of those planes crashing into the Twin Towers, knowing that normally those buildings were full of employees. And then to watch the Dow and the TSE fall like freight trains off a cliff. And then, with no end to the collapse of the markets in sight, the markets were halted.

The rest of the day was filled with news that all flights to the US were halted and ordered to land. I remember looking out of the building I was in and seeing a string of passenger jet aircraft lined up to land at St. John's airport. My team and I spent the day on the phone with clients, many of them crying.

The news and analysis continued and the markets were eventually re-opened. Then came the announcement of the war in Afghanistan.

This was followed by the "Axis of Evil" speech where Iraq was named by George Bush as being an ally of Al Qaeda. The rhetoric built throughout 2002 and on October 16, 2002 war with Iraq was authorized by the US Congress. This announcement short circuited any potential recovery. The Americans spent a long time trying to build consensus for the invasion and the delay kept the issue hanging over the markets. It certainly did not help that we also were also dealing with non-political matters including the fall of energy giant Enron and other frauds.

And the markets kept falling all the way from September 2001 to October 2002 when the headlines were truly dismal. See the headlines below.

Here is how October 1, 2002 greeted the world according to the *Globe and Mail*.

Illustration 29: Markets Suffer Dismal Quarter

And October 3rd brought this headline from the *Globe and Mail.*

Illustration 30: Mutual Fund Woes Continue

The "Mutual Fund Woes . . ." article discussed how $1.1 billion per month was coming out of mutual funds in Canada and that this was the 6th straight month of such redemptions.

This headline was followed by the *Wall Street Journal* on October 10, 2002.

Illustration 31: Blue Chips Tumble as Fundamental
Worries Hang Over the Markets

And the *Globe and Mail* published a similar article the same day discussing how blue chip stocks (supposedly the biggest and safest stocks) had been downgraded bringing the markets to new lows.

Illustration 32: Blue Chips Give Street the Blues

And those headlines were then followed on October 14, 2002 with an article from the *Globe and Mail* titled "Ten good reasons not to buy equities right now".

Illustration 33: Ten Good Reasons Not to Buy Equities Now

And by October 15 investors were trying to see if the markets had hit bottom but ". . . even some bulls have their doubts."

Illustration 34: Investors Trying to Decide if
Market Has Hit Bottom

The ten good reasons were indeed ten very good reasons to go with the herd, drown in the pessimism and wallow in the losses. The writer is indeed a learned man and it was hard to argue against his well thought out and logical article. I have little doubt that many people who read this article chose to sell at the time.

So extreme was the pessimism of the time that there was an article quoting the "Sage of the Market" in the *London Times* of England on October 17, 2002.

Illustration 35: Sage of the Market Sees Mother of All Crashes

This sage of the market was Robert Prechter who was on record as being one of the few public stock market commentators who had predicted the 1987 crash.

So, the logic was, if we should have believed Prechter in early 1987, which we should have, then we definitely should listen to him in October of 2002.

And what was Prechter forecasting in October 2002 when the market was already down some 40% and the Dow at 6000 from a peak at 11,000?

He was forecasting that the Dow was going to fall more than 5000 points further than it already had to settle below 1000 points. That would be an 83% fall from the current level at the time. This would bring the total market crash down more than 90% from its peak two and a half years before and would be a calamity beyond compare in western history.

The fear was palpable. Money was pouring out of mutual funds at the rate of over $1 billion a month for the six months ended October 2002. Analysts were "racing to the bottom" trying to outdo each other in downgrading one year targets on blue chip stocks.

We had ten good reasons not to buy stocks or stock funds.

Wow!

What had happened to all the great forecasts of June 2000? After enduring 40 months of market declines and relentlessly terrible news, how would you have felt seeing these headlines?

The 1990 invasion of Iraq was one thing but in October 2002 the Americans and British were talking about going to war in Iraq again and this time the world was certain (well, the Americans and British were) that Saddam Hussien had weapons of mass destruction which were either nuclear or chemical and here the Americans and British were going to try to take them away from him.

Of course, we all thought that he would use the weapons rather than lose them.

The market actually rose a bit after October 2002 but fell to new lows in April 2003 just as the Americans and British went ahead with the invasion itself.

It was interesting to note that from October 2002 to April 2003 when the markets were some 44% below the May/ August 2000 peak, more money was coming out of the mutual funds than any other time in history. Just check out this headline from the *Globe and Mail*, March 5 of 2003.

<u>Illustration 36: RRSP Season a Bust for Funds</u>

So, here we had the worst RRSP season in eight years. That is a sharp contrast to the RRSP season of 2000.

And I think this has to be the most understated headline from the *Globe and Mail* on March 15, 2003.

Illustration 37: "I Think People Are Getting Increasingly Pessimistic"

Then on April 3, 2003 the *Wall Street Journal* published this headline.

Illustration 38: War Expected to Sap Global Growth

And that Asia was not going to be a good place to invest.

Illustration 39: Forecasts for Asia Are Downgraded

While the *London Times* reported on the threat of a new recession on the same day.

Illustration 40: Threat of US Recession Grows

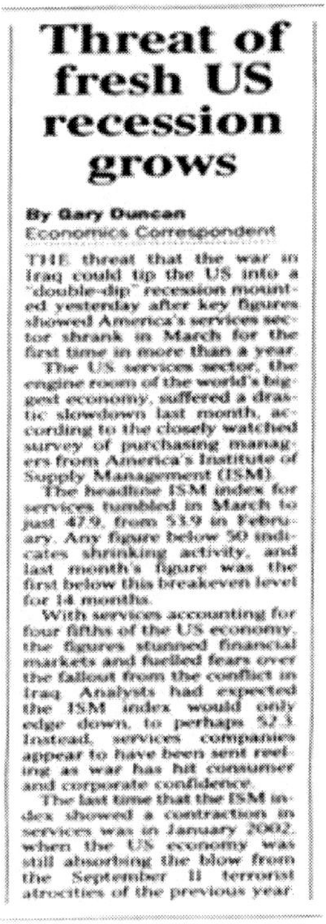

Threat of fresh US recession grows

By Gary Duncan
Economics Correspondent

THE threat that the war in Iraq could tip the US into a "double-dip" recession mounted yesterday after key figures showed America's services sector shrank in March for the first time in more than a year

The US services sector, the engine room of the world's biggest economy, suffered a drastic slowdown last month, according to the closely watched survey of purchasing managers from America's Institute of Supply Management (ISM).

The headline ISM index for services tumbled in March to just 47.9, from 53.9 in February. Any figure below 50 indicates shrinking activity, and last month's figure was the first below this breakeven level for 14 months.

With services accounting for four fifths of the US economy, the figures stunned financial markets and fuelled fears over the fallout from the conflict in Iraq. Analysts had expected the ISM index would only edge down, to perhaps 52.3. Instead, services companies appear to have been sent reeling as war has hit consumer and corporate confidence.

The last time the ISM index showed a contraction in services was in January 2002, when the US economy was still absorbing the blow from the September 11 terrorist atrocities of the previous year

This was reinforced by the *Wall Street Journal* reporting on worries about a weak economy on April 7, 2003.

Illustration 41: Jobs Data Suggest Weak Economy

Again, during the market decline interest rates were cut and capital injected into the markets in the same formula that had been used in the past to revive investor confidence.

We now know that no new recession came about in 2003 and China did not top out. In fact Asian funds soared and the markets in the US and Canada took a long time to recover but recover they did.

Since 2003 we have also had the Portus Hedge Fund fraud in Canada as well as Norburg, another fraud, which presaged Bernie Madoff in the US.

All of this culminated in the markets recovering again to all time record highs in 2008. It took a long time and we also now know that a lot of the money that came out of the dot com market in 2000 to 2002 ended up in real estate.

It is said that nature deplores a vacuum. Well, economics deplores a surplus of cash. This surplus arose when money came out of mutual funds and stock market investments and it tends to find an outlet, whether it be oil stocks, gold, technology or real estate. From 2002 on it went in to real estate and real estate related stocks including the banks throughout the world.

Until the summer of 2008.

Once again we had a market crash and and industry professionals saying this time is different.

But it wasn't.

Once again we had a debate in the US about setting up a Resolution Trust style institution and the bill was expected to be $700 billion or about twice as large as the last bank bailout in 1990. However the US economy is 71% larger than it was in 1990, which helps, at least a bit.

So again, interest rates were being cut and capital was being injected. The headlines looked the same. Only the name of the crisis had changed.

Looking back on all these crises we recognize that the best time to invest is when the markets have crashed and the headlines are miserable. In fact this is the only time you can buy low.

I want to repeat that.

You can only buy low when other investors want out.

They want out when headlines are miserable and worry is in the air. If you look back at the market bottoms you see that "10 Reasons Not to Buy Now" was one of the best days to buy. The only way you can sell high is when the opposite is true—when headlines are glorious and optimism prevails. "How Much More Good News Can an Investor Take" was actually a sell signal.

It is incredibly difficult to do this without proper experience and training. As we have seen by the headlines even the greatest minds in the business have trouble at market extremes.

I urge you to keep this book handy for when the next bubble arises or the next market plunge occurs. Check the headlines then against those in this chapter to see how close the headlines match. Then look after to see the next headline to see what happened last time.

This is the ride you have to get on again and again to retrain that gut feel brain and clear your head.

Apply, rinse and repeat.

Chapter 6

Consensus is Your Enemy

Remember how we discussed how most investors buy and sell at the wrong time and tend to do so in a herd mentality? That is, money moves into long term mutual funds, meaning Canadian, US and International stocks, *after* the market has risen and that money flows out of these investments *after* markets fall.

Is it any wonder why investors do this when the headlines are as bi-polar as we have seen in the review in the previous chapter. Now let's add one more factor.

The opinion of your investment advisor and his/her research team.

A chap by the name of Abe Cohen established Investor's Intelligence in 1963. (Any time I see someone who has such a long and successful history in our industry, I sit up and take notice. I also recognize that his information is very useful but even Abe is not perfect.)

What he found is that when markets fell, investment advisors became pessimistic and when they rose the advisors became optimistic. He used newsletter writers as the proxy for the overall opinions of the investment advisors and, in his case, recommended that clients sell when the percentage of optimistic (bullish) advisors exceeded a particular number and buy when the pessimism level (bearish) was at particularly low levels. (Source http://www.investorsintelligence.com/x/advisors_sentiment.html)

Consider this for a moment, you break your arm, you go to the hospital, and all of the doctors that you see agree that it should be put in a cast. Logic would dictate that you would follow their advice, and have a cast put on your arm. So, you go ahead and have a cast put on your arm. This is agreeing with the consensus.

This does not happen with investments—the consensus is often wrong.

That sounds almost ludicrous. It means that the advisor who does not agree with the commonly held beliefs of the day is the one you should hire to manage your money. How do you check one advisor against another in this circumstance? If you interview ten advisors and one of them disagrees with the other nine, how do you know he/she is the one you should follow?

There are a couple of ways to test this consensus. My favourite is called the cocktail party methodology. Unfortunately, it is not tax deductible but it is fun.

Under this methodology, you invite at least 30 people to a cocktail party (I did not say it was cheap and you need 30 people to get a good sample.) Then you do what one would normally do at a cocktail party but before the guests get to the point where they have to close one eye to write, ask them to write down in a note what they are investing in at that time. Then, order them taxis, send them home and call your advisor. Instruct him/her to do the opposite to what the group has done.

One caution: make sure that all of your guests have different investment advisors.

With any luck, this exercise (and this book) will turn you into a healthy skeptic. The technical term for a skeptic in our industry is a "Contrarian". Contrarians tend to have beliefs contrary to the popular beliefs at any particular point in time. They look at the above information from Investor's Intelligence, review headlines (good headlines cause worry, bad headlines means opportunity), as well as mutual fund sales (if investors are buying more bond funds than ever in history, is that an indication than you should sell?) and note where most new money is going and where the money is coming from. Contrarians look at the latest investment fads, the business commentary and the overall business climate. Then they invest in ignored areas, in sectors that are down and in investments no one wants. They use the front page of the newspaper as opportunities to sell and the back page as opportunities to buy.

One of my favourite simple research methods is to meet with various mutual fund company representatives and let them tell me their spiel. Their spiel is the story around the fund they wish to sell me and for me to sell to my clients that quarter. They usually have charts and graphs, historical numbers, and background on the sector, manager and fund.

Coincidentally the fund they are recommending most often happens to be the one with the best track record over the last one, three or five year period.

At the end of the spiel I ask how many meetings they have had on this fund in the last three months to see how many other advisors they have told this story to. This gives us an indication of how widespread the thinking is and, particularly with the larger fund companies, this indicates how predominant the consensus thinking is.

I compare the various reps stories to each other and generally find that they are all telling the same story about the same sector so that when high tech is running, the recommendation is high tech funds, when gold is running then the gold funds are recommended etc. We call this a theme and the theme is usually the "easy sell" at the time.

If you followed me so far you know that the "easy sell" tends to be the area to avoid in the long run. Be careful here—these themes can run for a good number of quarters so in the short run it may make money but they tend to do so with considerable risk.

I then throw the mutual fund reps a curve ball and ask which of their funds they are most embarrassed about. This often causes consternation for the rookie reps in particular because they are not used to such a question. When the answer to this question comes back from many reps to be in the same sector such as "our European fund is a dog" then a new theme appears. This tells us where the undervalued sector is. The more often and the longer that this message maintains, the more strongly I feel about investing in that theme.

You don't need mutual fund reps to access this information yourself. Ask your investment advisor about these conversations as part of your review and gauge them in light of the headlines of the day. Depending on how independent your advisor truly is this can be very entertaining, and potentially a great way to make money. Some advisors have to tow the company line while others can form their own opinions. This is a real test of your advisor.

For our purposes, just recognize that your advisor is as human as you are and subject to the same set of emotions, same input from the media, and is subject to the constraints imposed by his/her research department. Instead of managing one set of accounts, however, your advisor is managing the euphoria and the disappointment of many clients. And they are also seeing their own businesses rise and fall in value as the markets rise and fall. In our industry it is easier to be safe and propose the accepted general belief and be wrong than be a radical, preach against the generally expected views and risk not being right. Evidence suggests, however, that the latter opinion protects clients more and makes them more money. But to go against the grain is very, very difficult.

This is not an apology for your advisor's performance. It is, though, a recognition of the difficulty of the job. In order for your advisor to provide superior results he/she has to sell when you, the media, and often his/her own research department wants to buy and buy when these stakeholders want to sell. It is so much easier to simply follow the crowd. After all, who can blame the advisor who got it wrong like everyone else?

Not only is it easier to follow the crowd, in some firms the advisor cannot disagree with the firm's research department. They have to repeat the firm's recommendations and are not permitted to have an independent opinion.

In a number of instances this is a good thing because often the collective wisdom and experience of the firm is indeed better than that of an inexperienced advisor. The key discerning factor is how reasonable the conclusions are.

In order to keep ourselves humble (and this is an industry where we have a lot to be humble about) we all have to remember that you are paying your advisor to act as a more experienced filter on the market, standing between the great marketing machine and you. Of course, standing in between still means that you should expect your advisor be on your side.

Even so, it is incredibly difficult to go against the herd.

To give you some idea of how difficult it is to invest in a contrarian manner, consider that during the crash of 2008 after the market had fallen 55% from its peak, that only 13% of investors in Canada bought. This means a full 87% of investors either sold into the market lows or did nothing at all.

Do you not think that this is almost embarrassing that in a modern, information-rich, educated society where every hour of the 2008/2009 market collapse was documented and news of the low stock prices was forced in your face 24 hours a day that the majority of investors sold or did nothing?

The contrarian methodology flies in the face of Modern Portfolio Theory, which we will turn to after another healthy dose of skepticism.

Chapter 7

The Problem with Financial Plans and the Mountain Valley Wealth Management Solution

As discussed by Nassim Taleb in his book "*The Black Swan*", there is an unfortunate association between numbers and perceived accuracy. That is, when mathematical models are applied to any situation the numbers often become the focus of the exercise. With financial planning this gives the delusion of accuracy.

The delusion is created because the written plan certainly looks to be formal, often includes charts and graphs, and usually has projections and tax considerations. It often has conclusions refined to two decimal points. But how useful are these plans?

Most financial plans are prepared once and then never referred to again. The document is often used by advisors to attract new clients. This can be a problem. One ends up with a disassociated plan—one that is put on a shelf and gathers dust.

An alternative to such disassociated planning is the dynamic plan where your advisor is engaged as if they were your personal vice president of finance. In that relationship, you, the client, have an interactive discussion on a regular basis with the advisor so that not only do you set up a strategic long term plan initially, but you take tactical, short term positions along the way. It is kind of like a rolling plan, which is updated at least annually or when a major change happens in your life.

It is only when you have this level of discourse with your advisor that you maximize the benefit of having a professional investment advisor. You move beyond the simplified assumptions and employ him/her in everyday decisions.

In case you have not noticed, I tend to be more visual than number specific. I like charts and graphs rather than rows of numbers. Therefore I employ a chart as an alternative to a numerical financial plan. It is outlined below.

Illustration 42: Mountain Valley Retirement Plan

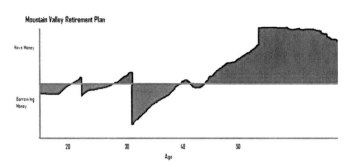

This chart, as crude as it is, consists of a series of mountains and valleys and can quickly give a bird's eye view of a client's financial situation and highlight the priorities that should be addressed. I call this the Mountain Valley illustration.

I have heard that a good investment advisor will cause the client to look down the road to see what is coming and plan accordingly but a great advisor will bring the client to the end of the road and cause the client to look back. The Mountain Valley Wealth Management Chart allows for such a look back.

I have simplified this greatly to show the pattern that most Canadians have to their wealth accumulation.

Age is displayed across the bottom and the left side is divided to indicate when you have money and when you do not. The horizontal flat line is the boundary.

We draw a mountain above the line when we have money, and we draw a valley below the line when we borrow. We end up with a money pattern.

From age zero to, really, about age 19, we borrow from our parents because we have no significant income and are incurring considerable expenses. As a child we need diapers, clothes, food, etc . . . Then we go through elementary school, middle school, high school and then potentially go to college or university—all we need is purchased as we borrow from our parents or obtain student loans.

Once we start in the work force we usually put ourselves as deep in debt as possible usually by borrowing money to buy a car. Only this time though we tend to borrow from a bank rather than our parents.

Over the next few years we may get a few more dollars here and there and may get a promotion or two and may meet another individual and decide to form a household with them. I have plotted this time period on the chart at age 28-ish.

We may decide to get married, or not, and we scramble a few dollars together and technically bankrupt ourselves by buying a house. So the mortgage on the house then has pushed us down on the chart deep into the valley and over the next few years we try to live life a bit and maybe start having children. And then the children start doing to us what we did to our parents when we were growing up.

So the next 18 to 19 years, usually into our late 30's and 40's, we are juggling between trying to pay off the mortgage, buying diapers, new cars, clothes for the kids, their education and then we get to the age somewhere in the late 40s and 50s when the children start to go to university or college. That can be like taking on a second mortgage because the cost is so high so we show the next valley after age 40.

Finally we reach a point in time, usually in our 50's, when the children have been raised and are now on their own, the house is paid off, and we are earning our highest income. Around that time we may receive an inheritance or possibly may have sold a business and that is the spike into the mountain after age 50.

As a consequence it's in their 50's that most individuals have money for investment for the first time. And of course when we hit our 50's the next thing we think about is retirement. So you are probably going to save and invest as much as possible in that phase of your life. And that tends to be when people start to look at the stock market for the first time. That is when they become investors and start making mistakes for the next 20 years until they are a wise and seasoned investor.

Once you understand this chart you can see how a financial plan should work. This chart is a great guide for you and your advisor to plot your own current position and see what you need to do to be where you will want to be in the future.

Your financial advisor's job is also to make the mountains taller and longer and your valleys shallower and shorter. The financial plan should address exactly that. You can also see when RESP's become needed, when term life insurance is required (to cover the cost of a deep valley) and the impact of paying off debt earlier. And you can see why many Canadians only start investing with vigor when they are around age 50.

One can also imagine how earning even a few percentage points more on your investments would make such a large difference to your savings over time. So one can see that financial planning is really about the attempt to move the whole chart up so that the mountains are higher and the valleys shallower.

Chapter 8

The Problem with Modern Portfolio Theory

"You cannot model human behaviour with mathematics."

Mike Gelband, Managing Director and Head of Global Fixed Income, Lehman Brothers as quoted in *A Colossal Failure of Common Sense; the collapse of Lehman Brothers* by Laurence G. MacDonald.

Modern Portfolio Theory (MPT) is the current foundation of the investment industry. It forms the basis for most financial planning for individuals and institutions and is employed by most financial planners and advisors in one form or another.

In our industry, if you do not employ Modern Portfolio Theory you face possible loss of your license and liability if an account falls in value. It is the "right thinking" method in our business.

The cries of the critics of this theory have been growing louder in the last number of years and as an investor or an advisor, you should be aware what this means to you.

So established is MPT that it forms the basis of licensing in our industry.

I had to study and pass a series of exams including the Canadian Securities Course, the Partners and Directors Course, the Options Course, Investment Management Techniques, the Branch Managers Course, the Portfolio Management Techniques Course and the Certified Financial Planners Exam to name just a few, in order to be licensed to practice as I do and that was after I received my Certified General Accountant (CGA) designation. All of these courses (except the CGA) are based on MPT to some degree or another.

You most likely encountered an application of MPT when you were asked to complete a questionnaire by your financial advisor or bank. One large part of preparing an investment plan for a client is determining the client's risk tolerance and this is an input to MPT.

Risk tolerance is normally determined by using a questionnaire which asks the client about their age, income, investment horizon, and how important particular attributes are to them. We take that risk tolerance profile and create a strategic asset allocation under MPT.

The fundamental assumption under MPT is that once we know your risk tolerance we can determine the optimal combination of stocks, bonds and cash for you, otherwise known as your asset allocation.

This is a matter of applying your risk score to a table and that table gives us the resulting optimal asset allocation.

However, there are at least three problems with Modern Portfolio Theory and to understand them we have to go back to where Modern Portfolio Theory began.

First, it should be pointed out that investment analysts under MPT today were called statisticians before MPT came around. The root of Modern Portfolio Theory (MPT) is in probability analysis and statistics. This is really important. We will come back to it later.

In 1952 Dr. Harry Markowitz, the father of Modern Portfolio Theory, was working for the Rand Corporation and began working on optimization techniques. He effectively plotted all combinations of stocks, bonds and cash versus variability over time and determined how each combination showed risk and return. We call this correlation analysis.

Essentially, he used samples of market returns (statistics) to establish a probability model of how markets moved up or down and how combinations of stocks, bonds, and cash moved with respect to the market. From this he derived the asset allocation principle.

This has further been developed to include correlation coefficients based on market cap (how large the company is), based on geography (Canadian stocks, US stocks, European stocks, Asian stocks and Emerging Markets stocks) and further diversified on investment style (growth managers versus value managers).

A correlation coefficient is a measure of how closely two investments move up or down together. This is useful because you generally want a number of investments that do not move together. In its most basic form bonds will generally move up when stocks fall and vice versa. Therefore by diversifying between stocks and bonds you will not lose everything when stocks fail or when interest rates rise and bonds fall. This is the basic diversification tenet.

According to MPT a properly balanced portfolio of stocks and bonds diversified geographically, by market size, and investment style would have a higher rate of return at a lower risk than a portfolio that did not use this approach.

Finally if we take portions of this money and place it into the hands of the best managers in each sector (the best value manager, the best growth manager, etc.), who are incredibly smart, educated, accredited with the proper investment licenses, and are experienced people who will buy only the best stocks and bonds and will sell those stocks and bonds when they are overpriced and buy them back when they are undervalued, we then have a pretty intelligent way to carefully handle clients' money.

The net result is an optimal combination for any client. MPT is an internally consistent theory that logically employs a very intelligent approach to investing that is easily explainable to a client.

Markowitz's work made a profound change to investment methodology of the time. It was a new paradigm and this paradigm is being followed by most regulatory organizations and industry participants today.

The theory has been developed further and used to determine the correlation of individual stocks to each other and the market, to price options and warrants, and most recently, to determine the price of derivatives including the value of subprime mortgages.

So profound and accepted is MPT that Markowitz, together with Merton M Miller and William F Sharpe, won the Nobel Prize in economics in 1990 for this work. Myron Scholes and Robert C Merton won the Nobel Prize for extension of the work in 1997. Other notable professionals in this field include Jack L. Treynor, Paul Samuelson, A. James Boness, Sheen T. Kassouf, Edward O. Thorp and Fisher Black.

These are some of the greatest minds in academic finance. Collectively they have set the archetype on how to invest clients in the modern world and they have taught the teachers—the Phd's and MBA's—who have gone on to create the textbooks for the investment industry and advise governments on setting up the regulations and laws in our industry.

Modern Portfolio Theory sets the standards that we must follow to manage our clients' money.

Pretty impressive, yes?

We have to add a couple of other tenets though.

One other tenet is that clients should "buy and hold". That is, clients and their advisors should not time the market. Timing the market is a term that means that you would sell when the market is up and buy when the market is down.

MPT and consequently many individuals in our industry are adamant that no one has ever successfully timed the market so, therefore, you should continue to hold your investments regardless of what the markets do.

Further, risk is reduced for clients who do not sell when the market is up by diversification of the underlying investment as noted above.

Mind you—you can and should "re-balance" your investments back to your original asset allocation when the markets run up significantly or fall dramatically. That is, if, according to your asset allocation, you should be 50% stock and 50% bond and the bond market takes off and you end up 60% bond and 40% stock, you should re-balance back to the original specifications of 50% stock and 50% bond but we will soon see how much of a difference that such rebalancing makes.

I have always had some difficulty with the actual application of Modern Portfolio Theory because of what I see as certain assumptions that have no basis in reality. Other writers have more than just a bit of difficulty. They are convinced that Modern Portfolio Theory is a complete waste of time and money.

First, Modern Portfolio Theory was created for institutions such as pension funds but not for individuals. The difference is that institutions have infinite lives, while individuals do not and this shows up in the model when we try to employ it.

Institutions can wait out market downturns knowing that eventually the logic of Modern Portfolio Theory may prevail but humans have more immediate needs. Individual clients cannot afford to wait as long as pension funds and other institutions. Three years is a long time to have your account down and ten years is completely unacceptable for a retiree while for institutions, it is an aggravation but not a crisis.

Second, Markowitz assumed that risk was equal over time, which it is, but risk is not equal at every point in time.

This is important. If twin investors, identical in every way, complete the same risk tolerance survey, one during a time when the market was at a peak, such as the summer of 1987, and the other at a market trough such as October 1987 when the market was down 47%, they will end up with the identical asset allocation meaning they will have the same proportion of stock in their accounts.

This is just wrong.

After a market has fallen risk is much lower than when a market is at a peak. This means that one of the twins should have a lot more stock than the other but Modern Portfolio Theory does not dictate this.

And finally, the entire reason that we employ Modern Portfolio Theory is to reduce risk but unfortunately, it breaks down completely when you need it most. It does not work when there is market panic. When those events occur there is no place to hide or, as some advisors put it, all correlations go to one. This means everything moves together in the same direction, which is down.

This is exactly what happened in the crashes of 1987, in 1990, in 1998, in 2000 and in 2008.

Modern Portfolio Theory appears to have relevance to some degree when markets are not in panic mode, either because it really works or because all the market players agree that it works and abide by it but it does not protect when it is needed the most.

This is like buying a fire suppression system for your house but finding out it only works when the fires are small. A big fire, large enough to burn down the whole house, causes the fire suppression to fail.

I may disagree with MPT but two other very noteworthy critics have expressed stronger opinions.

In June, 2008 Justin Fox released *The Myth of the Rational Market (HarperCollinsCanada, 2008)* He does an excellent job of reviewing the history and development of MPT while cutting out the jargon and the math.

One of his observations, among many others, is that MPT may very well be based on statistical theory but there are not enough observations of the market for a proper statistical sample to be obtained. In statistics, the size of the sample is vital. If the number of observations is not large enough then you cannot rely on any of the conclusions.

This is like saying that there are 33 million people in Canada but I only interviewed 12 in British Columbia and all of them are voting NDP therefore the NDP will form the next Federal Government.

It is also like trying to put together a mortality table, which is based on statistics, for an insurance company and having records of the death of only 5 people. The sample size is too small.

Simply put, he concludes that Modern Portfolio Theory is indeed (are we surprised?) a myth.

A more blunt and aggressive review of MPT was authored by Nassim Nicholas Taleb in his book *The Black Swan (Random House Publishing Group, 2010)* We talked about him in the chapter on having two minds about investing.

The Black Swan is terribly difficult to read and I think it was made so intentionally. Taleb has reached something of a cult status where he is delighted to anger the supporters of MPT and is known to ignore a question at a seminar if he deems it too stupid for him to bother answering it.

He has pointed out that Myron Scholes and Robert C. Merton, two of the individuals who had been named as Nobel Prize winners and key proponents of MPT, unsuccessfully put their theory into practice through a company called Long Term Capital Management (LTCM). The company faltered in 1998 during the Asian currency crises and was actually blamed for making the crises worse than it would have otherwise become. LTCM had to be bailed out by the U.S. government in 1998.

Myron Scholes and Robert C. Merton plus their investors lost billions of dollars.

How embarrassing is that? I mean, really? Myron Scholes and Robert C. Merton were THE experts on the planet, had won the Nobel Prize in economics, and have textbooks written and laws put in place for the entire industry and they could not make any money from their own advice?

Kinda sounds like a bald guy trying to sell you a cure for baldness.

Consider another industry—how about engineering? Let's say that the lead engineer in the world built a bridge and it fell apart. Wouldn't a few questions arise?

LTCM started out modestly but with the attraction caused by having such extraordinary names as Scholes and Merton with their Nobel prizes in tow, the company blossomed and grew quickly. After all, wouldn't you want your money managed by a Nobel prize winning genius or two?

To amplify their earnings, LTCM borrowed heavily and invested that into the market according to their beliefs. By the time of the 1998 Asian Currency crises LTCM had become so large and involved in so many markets that its failure in 1998 was thought to be a threat that would worsen the international currency crises and bring down more companies and maybe even some nations.

Consequently, the Federal Reserve of New York organized a bailout of LTCM by its creditors leaving Myron Scholes, Robert C. Merton and the other partners, who had put $1.9 billion of their own money in, with nothing. Long Term Capital Management did not live up to its name and was liquidated in 2000.

On Taleb's webpage one can see the efforts he is making to expose those that advocate Modern Portfolio Theory to the point that he calls them "charlatans", recommends that business schools be closed and that supporters of business schools withdraw their funding.

Pretty harsh—but, wait—there's more.

Taleb has met with the King of Sweden, home of the Nobel Prizes, to pressure him for a revocation of the Nobel prize for economics. He wants Merton, Scholes, Markowitz and others to be forced to give the money back as well as their Nobel Prizes in Economics.

Even more extreme is his article on his web page titled:

The Black Swan: Quotes & Warnings that the Imbeciles Chose to Ignore

Kinda subtle, isn't he?

The book *The Black Swan* was published in April 2007 and predicted the market decline of 2008 based on the risks Taleb saw in MPT application throughout the investment world. Unlike the Nobel Prize winning Scholes and Merton, Taleb has also made a tremendous amount of money for himself and his clients putting his theory of non-MPT into practice.

Remember when we discussed the 1987 stock market crash and how one trader had shorted the market when others had not and thereby made a fortune as the market fell? Taleb intentionally did the same thing in 1998, 2000 and 2008.

Taleb makes the case, as does Justin Fox in *The Myth of the Rational Market*, that the weakness in Modern Portfolio Theory lies in the assumption that you can apply statistical methods to predict the markets. If that simple assumption is wrong then the whole theory is flawed but whereas Fox says the problem is that there is not enough of a history of the market to take a statistical sample, Taleb says the problem is even worse.

For those who are mathematically inclined or can tolerate the punishment of Taleb's writing style, by all means check out his books. I love them because they are mentally challenging and he pushes me beyond my comfort level, forcing me to backtrack often and pull out mathematics and concepts I have not seen in years. In several instances he digs into Chaos theory and I have little doubt that at some point in the future he will be knee deep into quantum mechanics in an effort to explain market fluctuations. But I find his books challenging in the same way that I admire some charged particle physicists talking about charm, and the up and down quark.

For those who would not find Taleb interesting I want to save you the time from reading his books, so here's his punch line:

The distribution of investment returns is not Gaussian because it does not have a bell curve distribution that traditional statistics employs. Instead the distribution is Mandelbrotian because it has a fractal distribution, much the same way as plants grow and chaos develops.

That was painful. Sorry—I will not do that again.

More importantly, what does this mean for you the investor and your investment advisor?

This questions whether the book learnin' that investment advisors, analysts and their firms are employing is indeed correct. We can question MPT through the analysis of Justin Fox, Nassim Nicholas Taleb and others but my mind works in a simpler manner.

Simply put: What have been the results of investment managers' returns to clients over time.

I mean, enough with the theory. We know the theory has been employed by just about every investment fund and advisor out there.

Show me the money! What have been the bottom line results? Have clients made money from the application of this theory?

This brings us to our next chapter and the one I think may be the most surprising.

Chapter 9

Modern Portfolio Theory Results

We began this book with the following slides:

Illustration 43: Results of Investor Behaviour

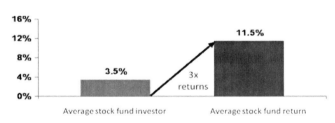

RESULTS OF INVESTOR
BEHAVIOUR

1984 – 2003

Sources: Dalbar Inc. and Lipper Inc.

Illustration 44: Gain On $1000 Invested in 1984

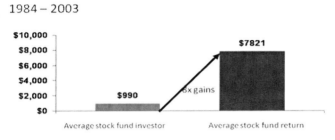

GAIN ON $1000 INVESTED IN 1984

1984 – 2003

Sources: Dalbar Inc. and Lipper Inc.

And we talked about how this was US data but there is evidence that Canadian investors are behaving the same as Americans so it is reasonable to believe that Canadian investors are having the same results.

Again, these charts show that investors are not earning as much as the average underlying fund is earning. In the first part of the book we showed that this situation arose because investors tend to buy at the peak of the market and sell at the bottom of the market.

The intention of the first part of the book was to change the behaviour of investors so that they could earn the same returns that the average fund is earning. That change alone could make a monumental difference in the returns that the average client could earn over time.

Now here's the kicker:

What if I told you that the average mutual fund is not earning as much as the underlying index?

That is, you could earn a higher rate of return than even the average fund if you invested in the index rather than a regular mutual fund.

If you are a little confused, don't worry about it. Let me explain this a bit more.

Traditionally, investment advisors have selected mutual funds because of the tenets of Modern Portfolio Theory.

Modern Portfolio Theory is a logical, well studied and intelligent theory to investing money for clients and when you hear about how it is put together it certainly seems to make sense.

That is, telling a client that we are going to use methodologies developed by Nobel prize winning economists and employ well educated, highly experienced investment managers throughout the world to find the best stocks, to monitor your holdings, and to sell those stocks when the time is right sounds like a pretty sensible approach.

As advisors, in addition to guidance on tax reduction strategies, estate planning, and other services we provide, we are supposed to guide clients to make the most money by using the best tools available.

We have two basic choices.

1) We can place clients into a stock and/or bond market index.

2) We can place clients into a traditional mutual fund that employs Modern Portfolio Theory.

(Note well—we can also use pension fund managers, hedge funds, individual stocks, etc but let's keep this simple.)

Well, the best way to check out which selection is better is to have an independent expert look at these two choices and that is exactly what we are going to present here.

We will look at the report cards of those funds using Modern Portfolio Theory, which in the report that follows are called Actively Managed Funds, and compare those returns to their respective underlying indices.

Understand that if you have a Canadian equity fund that equity fund is selecting its investments from the companies that make up the TSE Index, which is the index. So, I could recommend that you select a fund manager to do this (an Active Manager) or I could recommend that I just buy the index for you.

Similarly, if you are interested in dividend funds, we can compare the dividend funds to the dividend index. And so on.

Standard and Poors is the "independent expert" we are going to rely on to help us judge which is better for you the client.

Standard and Poors is a US based company that has been giving independent evaluations on various investments, such as ratings on corporate and government bonds, for many years. Their credibility is quite high.

Here are the report cards compiled by Standard and Poors.

On June 4, 2009 Standard and Poors published their latest report to that point in time called SPIVA which means "Standard and Poor's Indices Versus Actives". If you search that word on the web the report will pop up.

This is the ultimate report card for traditional, actively managed mutual funds.

First, let's put the report in perspective:

Here is a graph of the Toronto Stock Exchange with an arrow showing were the market was in March 2009

Illustration 45: Returns to the Bottom of the Market in 2009

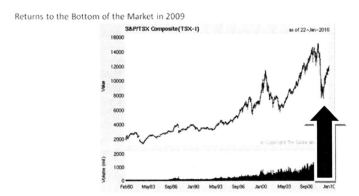

Returns to the Bottom of the Market in 2009

So, you can see on the chart the five year period ending March 2009:

Here is the front page of the SPIVA report for the five years ending March 31, 2009.

Illustration 46: Standard & Poor's Index Versus Active Funds Scorecard For Canadian Funds

STANDARD
&POOR'S

June 4, 2009

Analytical Contacts

SPIVA Canada Scorecard
[illegible]

SPIVA Methodology
[illegible]

Media Contacts

[illegible]

Index Versus Active Funds Scorecard For Canadian Funds

Standard & Poor's Indices Versus Active Funds Scorecard for Q1 2009

- The Standard & Poor's Indices Versus Active Funds (SPIVA) Scorecard reports performance of actively managed Canadian mutual funds corrected for survivorship bias and shows equal and asset weighted peer averages.
- **Domestic Equities:** For the first quarter of 2009, only 27.4% of Canadian Equity active funds were able to outperform the S&P/TSX Composite Index. In contrast, active funds in the Canadian Small/Mid Cap Equity category fared better with 70.4% beating the S&P/TSX Completion Index. Similarly, for the Canadian Focused Equity category 76.9% of active funds outpaced the blended index (comprised of 50% S&P/TSX Composite + 25% S&P 500 + 25% S&P EPAC LargeMidCap).
- Over the past twelve months, actively managed Canadian Equity, Canadian Small/Mid Cap Equity and Canadian Focused Equity equal weighted returns are lower than their benchmarks: the S&P/TSX Composite Index, the S&P/TSX Completion Index and the blended S&P/TSX Composite Index respectively. Returns of the aforementioned indices exceeded active fund's equal weighted returns in these categories by 0.6%, 1.2% and 0.9% respectively.
- Over longer periods, we continue to observe indices outperforming the majority of domestic active funds. In three-year and five-year periods, only 24.7% and 8.4%, respectively, of actively managed Canadian Equity funds have outperformed the S&P/TSX Composite Index. In three-year period, only 42.4% of active funds in the Canadian Dividend & Income Equity category beat the S&P/TSX Dividend Aristocrats Index. In the five-year period no active funds were able to beat this index.
- **Foreign Equities:** In Q1 2009, 73.3% of active funds in the International Equity category, 82.0% in the Global Equity category, and 56.6% in the U.S. Equity category have outpaced S&P EPAC LargeMidCap, S&P Developed LargeMidCap and S&P 500 indices respectively.

It is a bit hard to read so here is a summary:

Illustration 47: It's Hard to Consistently Beat the Markets

It's Hard to Consistently Beat the Markets

5 years ending Q1 2009

- Canadian Equity
  - Only 8.4% of active managers outperformed Benchmark index
  - Survivorship rate of only 44.9%
- US Equity
  - Only 11.0% of active managers outperformed Benchmark index
  - Survivorship rate of only 41.0%
- International Equity
  - Only 11.1% of active managers outperformed Benchmark index
  - Survivorship rate of only 58.7%
- Global Equity
  - Only 15.5% of active managers outperformed Benchmark index
  - Survivorship rate of only 42.3%

Source: Standard & Poor's Index Versus Active Funds Scorecard For Canadian Funds (SPIVA) for Q1 2009

The report shows that for the five years ending March 2009, which was the bottom of the stock market crash of 2008 that only 8% (rounded) of actively managed funds outperformed the TSE index.

I then looked at their report for the five years ended at the peak of the market which was June 2008.

Again here is the chart of the TSE so you can see that the previous five years were some of the most positive years in history.

<u>Illustration 48: What About Active Managers Versus the / Index to the Top of the Market in 2008?</u>

What about Active Managers versus the /Index to the top of the market in 2008?

Illustration 49: Underperformance of Active Versus Index

STANDARD &POOR'S

Sep 3, 2008

Index Versus Active Funds Scorecard For Canadian Funds

Standard & Poor's Indices Versus Active Funds Scorecard for Q2 2008

Analytical Contacts

SPIVA Canada Scorecard
Jasmit Bhandal
(416) 507 3203
jasmit_bhandal@sandp.com

SPIVA Methodology
Srikant Dash
(212) 438 3012
srikant_dash@sandp.com

Media Contacts

Dave Guarino
(212) 438 1471
dave_guarino@sandp.com

❏ The Standard & Poor's Indices Versus Active Funds (SPIVA) Scorecard reports performance of actively managed Canadian mutual funds corrected for survivorship bias and shows equal and asset weighted peer averages.

❏ **Domestic Equities:** For the second quarter of 2008 only 31.2% of Canadian Equity active managers were able to outperform the S&P/TSX Composite Index. Active managers in the Canadian Small/Mid Cap Equity category fared better with 57.7% beating the S&P/TSX Completion Index. In the Canadian Focused Equity category 51.7% of active managers outpaced the blended index (comprised of 50% S&P/TSX Composite + 25% S&P 500 + 25% S&P/Citigroup EPAC PMI).

❏ Over the past twelve months, actively managed Canadian Equity, Canadian Small/Mid Cap Equity and Canadian Focused Equity equal weighted returns are lower than their benchmarks: the S&P/TSX Composite Index, the S&P/TSX Completion Index and blended S&P/TSX Composite Index respectively. Returns of the aforementioned indices exceeded active manager's equal weighted returns in these categories by 6.3%, 3.1% and 0.3% respectively.

❏ In stark contrast to Q1 2008, Canadian Small/Cap Cap Equity active funds performed much better this period. The majority beat the S&P/TSX Completion Index in Q2 2008 and equal and asset weighted returns for the period, were higher amongst active funds than the index.

❏ **Foreign Equities:** In Q2 2008, 31.8% of active managers in the International Equity category, 55.9% in the Global Equity category, and 51.2% in the U.S. Equity category have outpaced S&P/Citigroup EPAC PMI, S&P/Citigroup World PMI and S&P 500 indices respectively.

I know it is difficult to read so here is the summary:

Illustration 50: Summary: Underperformance of Active Versus Index

Underperformance of Active Versus Index

SPIVA Report – Active Managers who Beat the Index

Asset Class	1Yr	3Yr	5Yr	Total Return Benchmarks
Canadian Equity	15.15%	11.58%	6.03%	S&P/TSX* Capped Composite Index TR
Canadian Small Cap	25.46%	-	-	S&P/TSX Completion Index TR
U.S. Equity	44.94%	14.09%	12.43%	S7P 500 Index TR C$

Source: Standard & Poors, as of June 30, 2008

- Adjusted for survivorship bias
- Pre-tax results
- Corrected Benchmark Indices

It turned out that only 6% (rounded) of the traditional, actively managed funds beat the indices during the previous five years to the peak in the market in 2008.

But what about risk? There has been discussion that often Actively Managed Funds fall less than the indices when markets fall.

One of the longest and deepest market corrections occurred from the market peak of August 2000 to December 2003. Below is the chart of the TSE showing the collapse from the down arrow (August 2000) to the market bottom indicated by the up arrow (April 2003).

Illustration 51: S&P Research on Active Managers Versus the Index August 2000 to the Market Bottom April 2003

Standard and Poors did a special report for this period and published it on August 5, 2008:

Illustration 52: Standard & Poor's Index Versus Active Funds Scorecard For Canadian Funds

STANDARD &POOR'S

Aug 5, 2008

Index Versus Active Funds Scorecard For Canadian Funds

Standard & Poor's Indices Versus Active Funds
Bear Market Report (Aug 2000 – Dec 2002)

Analytical Contacts

SPIVA Canada Scorecard
Jasmit Bhandal
(416) 507 3203
jasmit_bhandal@sandp.com

SPIVA Methodology
Srikant Dash
(212) 438 3012
srikant_dash@sandp.com

Media Contacts

Dave Guarino
(212) 438 1471
dave_guarino@sandp.com

❏ The Standard & Poor's Indices Versus Active Funds (SPIVA) Scorecard compares performance of actively managed Canadian mutual funds (corrected for survivorship bias) with performance of relevant benchmark indices.

❏ This special edition of SPIVA follows the Canadian market from a peak in August 2000 through to the trough in December 2002 to analyze the effects of a bear market on active versus passive performance.

Domestic Equities:

❏ Many people believe that actively managed funds perform better than indices during bear markets. However:

- From the August 2000-December 2002 period, only 38.9% active Canadian Equity funds outperformed the S&P/TSX Capped Composite Index.
- Canadian Equity funds exceeded the S&P/TSX Capped Composite return on an equal and asset weighted basis; this reflects the strong performance of only a few funds.
- The majority of Canadian equity funds still underperformed the index reflecting the high degree of active risk.
- Only 34.4% of active Large Cap Equity funds were able to beat the large cap S&P/TSX 60 Capped Index.
- The S&P/TSX SmallCap Index outperformed 70% of active Small Cap Canadian Equity funds.

Foreign Equities:

❏ During the same period, only 29% of active U.S. Equity funds were able to outpace the S&P 500.

❏ International Equity active funds present a similar picture with only 32% beating the S&P/Citigroup EPAC PMI Index.

❏ The S&P/Citigroup World PMI Index outperformed 54.1% of active funds in the Global Equity fund space.

It turns out that only 34% (rounded) of large cap Canadian Equity Funds fell less than the S&P/TSX Composite during that period. This means that 66% of the funds fell more than the overall market.

So, 6.03% of mutual funds did better than the index in one five year period and 8.4% outperformed in another five year period. Let's give the managers a break and round up to say that 9% of managers provide our clients with better returns than if we put the clients' money into the index directly.

Then, I thought, maybe we should only deal with that small 9% of managers.

Unfortunately, there is a problem with that as can be seen on the slide below:

<u>Illustration 53: Why Picking Today's Hot Manager Isn't the Solution</u>

Why picking today's hot manager isn't the solution

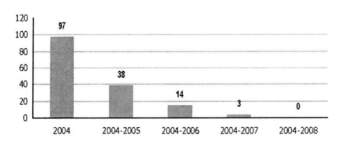

Managers in the top 25% for consecutive years: 2004 - 2008

Source: Morningstar Canada, 2004-2008
In 2008, none of the original 97 managers from 2004 had remained in the top 25% every year since 2004

This study obtained from Morningstar Research shows that the managers that outperformed the index in the previous 5 years are not likely to be the managers that outperform the index in the next five years.

So, here we have a problem, both from the Modern Portfolio Theory side and from the investment advice side.

If Modern Portfolio Theory is indeed the "right thinking" paradigm and is the required practice in our industry by which investments are selected and risk minimized for clients here is evidence that it is not working.

From an advisor's point of view, we have a duty of care to tell clients about the faults of Modern Portfolio Theory and the alternatives of Hedge Funds, Index ETF's and the tools that the author of *The Black Swan* employs.

It also means that we need to control risk in investing in some other manner than the current Modern Portfolio Theory paradigm provides. It means that we have to adapt new techniques including some form of the tools that Taleb employs.

We cannot use only Taleb's tools because many investment advisors do not have the licenses to employ them, many clients are not sophisticated enough to understand them, and they profit only when markets crash. A rising market will cause Taleb's followers to lose money.

On a larger scale though, this discussion properly calls into question the traditional buy and hold approach to investing, which investors have been questioning anyway. Afterall, from 1998 to 2008 Canadians experienced three major market crashes. As the boomers get older and closer to retirement they wonder if they can survive another crash and are demanding better risk protection.

An analysis of the top 10 largest equity mutual funds in Canada revealed that the average stock based mutual fund fell 44% when the market fell in 2008. Even balanced funds fell over 20%. Investors want better protection than that.

This is a radical change, there will be much resistance to change, and it will take some time before the industry adapts.

Resistance will arise for a number of reasons. One of the benefits of MPT has been that it made an investment advisor's job a lot easier. Investment Advisors had assigned the money management job to mutual funds. This allowed advisors to focus on gathering new clients and is one of the reasons that the average advisor in Canada deals with 253 families (*Investment Executive, September 2009*).

It is also easy to "sell" a mutual fund because showing a client the history of the fund, outlining the education, credentials and experience of the managers is a process that often sells the fund. Fund companies have already prepared this information for the advisor. For the client it seems to make sense.

In many cases all clients of an Investment Advisors are placed with one or two mutual fund companies. This wholesale investment solution is fast and easy to implement.

If an advisor decides to take back the investment management function from the mutual fund companies it means that the advisor will have to deal with smaller numbers of clients and they will need new licenses to employ non-traditional techniques.

From the mutual fund companies point of view this is disastrous. Most mutual funds are called traditional or "long only" funds meaning they can hold (go long) stock but not short (sell more than they own when they believe the market will fall). Advisors have been the primary source of traditional mutual fund's business and as the non-traditional techniques become more commonplace these funds may see money come out of them.

Chapter 10

An Additional Problem—The Nifty 44: The Hollowing Out of the Toronto Stock Exchange

There is another problem to make you aware of.

Remember we said that US and Canadian mutual funds were generally the same? Well, we have a problem that the Americans don't.

It turns out Canadians are running out of stocks.

Since the 1990's the number of large Canadian stocks listed on the Toronto Stock Exchange (the TSX) have diminished. In the recent past we would refer to the TSE 300 (the largest 300 stocks) but some of those 300 stocks are now pretty small.

Consider the following partial list of companies that existed before 1990 and have disappeared since 1990:

Nortel	Nova Scotia Power	Newbridge Networks
Noranda	Confederation Life	Laidlaw
Cominco	Royal Trust	Loewen Group
Inco	Standard Trust	Abitibi
Alcan	Corel	
NB Tel	Newfoundland Telephone	

Now this is only a partial list and we have had new companies emerge including RIM and Potash but still the number of large Canadian companies is less now then it was in 1990.

At the same time, the size of the individual mutual funds and the amount of dollars invested in mutual funds in Canada has grown dramatically.

This is causing a problem.

This point was first highlighted by Eric Bushell of CI Mutual Funds. Eric is an award winning mutual fund manager and is managing collectively about $4 billion worth of mutual funds.

Eric discussed how he, and other Canadian mutual fund managers that invest in the largest companies on the Toronto stock exchange, could invest in no more than 44 of Canada's largest companies.

Now, this is a surprise.

Turns out he is right and there are several reasons that these managers can only invest in what I have called the Nifty 44. (There used to be a Nifty 50 at one point on the US market in the late 1960's. I have borrowed that phrase here.)

One reason for limiting trading to only 44 companies is that the 45th company has too little daily trading volume for Eric and other managers to easily get into or out of the stock as they see fit.

(Daily Trading Volume: The number of shares traded in a day. If you want to buy or sell 1,000,000 shares in one day will you push the price of the stock up or down significantly? If the answer is yes, there is not enough daily trading volume and you should not buy the stock.)

The second factor is the overall capitalization value of the company. That is, if the number of shares times the price of the stock is less than a certain figure, buying a meaningful position in that stock may be impossible.

For example, let's say you are managing a balanced fund, a dividend fund, an income fund, a large cap fund and a general equity fund for one firm, and that these funds total something close to $20 billion. If you put 5% of your money into a single company that means you invest $1 billion. But what if the company is only worth $5 billion in total? You then own 20% of the company and then you have to declare ownership and intention and meet certain restrictive regulatory requirements. If that was not your intention then problems could arise, particularly when you try to sell.

So, this problem means that you, as an investment manager, have your hands tied to those 44 or so large stocks.

But wait—there's more. (Or less, depending on how you view this problem.)

If you are restricted to only the largest 44 stocks does this mean that effectively your fund has become an index fund? There is an index called the S&P\TSX 60. It is comprised of the largest 60 companies on the Toronto stock exchange so if you are buying 44 of the largest 60 how close will your performance track the index itself?

The problem is the difficulty of adding value as a manager over the S&P\TSX 60 index and doing so at a reasonable fee.

That is, what is the chance that you can provide a higher return to clients than if the clients just invested in the index?

So still with the Nifty 44, what happens when you stay with those 44 stocks and the market starts to fall? If all the large mutual fund managers are also restricted to only those 44 stocks then you may have a wave of sellers with no buyers. Such things market crashes are made of.

One of the means that Eric Bushell is employing to get around the Nifty 44 problem is to move away from the Canadian market and place some of the billions he is investing outside Canada. Of course, this means he is no longer running a purely Canadian fund, which many Canadians want, and introduces currency risk to the client, which many Canadians do not want, but it is one potential solution.

More than likely many more fund managers will be considering moving in this direction in the future, and so they should.

And maybe so should you. Canadian funds have been top performers in the past few years but there is no guarantee that will continue. After all, our market underperformed for many years and we really only have three sectors we can invest in if we restrict our investments to Canada—energy, financial, and materials. We have almost no pharmaceutical sector, little manufacturing, a small amount of retail, little high tech, etc.

To properly diversify we need to invest in sectors that do not exist in Canada and we have to go international to invest in those sectors.

For Canadian investors, one needs to be aware of these restrictions.

Suffice it to say that this is a topic that should be discussed with your financial advisor.

Chapter 11

The Death of Buy and Hold?

We briefly touched on whether Buy and Hold is a valid investment principle in a previous chapter. Here we will discuss this concept in more detail.

The Buy and Hold investment philosophy advocates that investment advisors should keep their clients invested in the market at all times because it is impossible to determine when is the best time to get out of the market and the best time to re-enter the market. Further, there is evidence that the number of "up days" in a market cycle are so few that missing just 40 of the best days over a 10 year period could significantly reduce your earnings on your investments.

On the page below you will see a chart of the Toronto Stock Exchange dating back to 1980.

Illustration 54: S&P / TSX Composite (TSX-1)

It is pretty clear from the chart of the exchange that from 1980 to 1998 the market went up roughly 13% per year with only two major market corrections—1980 and 1987—during that period of time.

We had some difficult periods and a lot of worries as we discussed in the previous chapters, but fundamentally by following the chart you can see that a Buy and Hold investment philosophy could be considered to be a sound philosophy from 1980 to 1998. According to Lloyd Williams, industry-renowned advisor to the advisors, it was during the 1980 to 1998 period that Modern Portfolio Theory became the accepted paradigm, because it worked well during that time.

From 1998 to 2008, a ten-year period, we've had three crashes whereas in the previous 18 years we only had two. In addition to that, the extent of the crashes in the last ten years have been more severe and it appears that the amplitude of the market is increasing. That is, the height at which the markets recover after a crash is higher than the previous highs and the following market drop brought us back down to where the market was in 1998. Something seems to have fundamentally changed and the Buy and Hold strategy has not provided the returns hoped for since 1998.

There are a number of theories as to what has changed. One theory was presented back in 1996 by an analyst named Jim Allworth. Mr. Allworth was employed with RBC Dominion Securities as a strategist and in 1996 he talked about how long-term interest rates were falling back to levels not seen since the 1960's. Now the long-term interest rates he was talking about were those on Government of Canada and US Government bonds maturing between 20 and 30 years from 1996.

So back in 1996 interest rates were falling, they had peaked in 1981 at 18% in Canada and 16% in the United States, and then fell and were approaching 6% in 1996 through 1997. Mr. Allworth's presentation to RBC Dominion Securities advisors at the time was about how the world would look different once that this 6% level was reached. This was a very profound presentation because what he suggested was that one of the reasons why stock markets in both countries had gone up so much and so steadily since 1980 was related to the high interest rates of the late 1970's through to 1981.

Once those rates started to fall in 1980 and 1981 money starting coming out of the bond market and into the stock market. However, once interest rates hit that 6% level the rate of money coming out of the bond market and into the stock market would slow and this smaller flow of money would mean that a different market pattern would result.

As an illustration of his forecast, Mr. Allworth put up a chart of the New York Stock Exchange from 1956 to 1974. During that period of time long term interest rates were at or below 6%. I have created a chart covering the same period on the following page here.

<u>Illustration 55: Dow Jones 1959-1974 Source: BigCharts.com</u>

We can clearly see that from 1956 to 1974, a period of 15 years, the New York Stock Exchange went through a series of gyrations and ended up at the same level in 1974 as it was in 1956.

Now, be aware that from 1980 to 1998 the stock markets did rise pretty consistently and a buy-and-hold philosophy yielded excellent results. Many investors and advisors generally assumed that stock markets would always rise because that had been their most recent experience up to 1998. Regardless of the evidence since 1998 many people still hold on to that assumption.

In fact, whether his theory was correct or whether he has just been lucky, since 1998 the markets have gone sideways, in keeping with Mr. Allworth's forecast of 1996.

As a consequence, the statement that Buy and Hold is the best strategy may in fact not be correct. It certainly has to be questioned.

One other factor also arises—we are back to the investor behaviour problem. Remember, most investors buy at the worst possible time, usually after the market has risen and optimism is in the air. Consequently, a buy and hold strategy put in place at or near a market peak will provide disastrous results, maximum worry for the investor, and incredible frustration for all concerned.

There is only one real time that buy and hold has worked and it is incredibly difficult to do. Let's talk about why next.

Chapter 12

Who's Afraid of a Recession?

Before we start talking about solutions we have to address a number of other assumptions and behaviours of investors and advisors.

Well, apparently everyone is afraid of recessions. Should you be?

It should be apparent at this point that most investors make new investments during boom times, when markets are surging higher, when we have had a "bull run", and the economic measures are reporting positive results.

And it should be apparent that most investors sell when we are in a recession. In fact, the fear of a recession is a prime worry of most investors and certainly of the investment media.

Illustration 56: Threat of Fresh US Recession Grows

Threat of fresh US recession grows

By Gary Duncan
Economics Correspondent

THE threat that the war in Iraq could tip the US into a "double-dip" recession mounted yesterday after key figures showed America's services sector shrank in March for the first time in more than a year.

The US services sector, the engine room of the world's biggest economy, suffered a drastic slowdown last month, according to the closely watched survey of purchasing managers from America's Institute of Supply Management (ISM).

The headline ISM index for services tumbled in March to just 47.9, from 53.9 in February. Any figure below 50 indicates shrinking activity, and last month's figure was the first below this breakeven level for 14 months.

With services accounting for four fifths of the US economy, the figures stunned financial markets and fuelled fears over the fallout from the conflict in Iraq. Analysts had expected the ISM index would only edge down, to perhaps 52.3. Instead, services companies appear to have been sent reeling as war has hit consumer and corporate confidence.

The last time that the ISM index showed a contraction in services was in January 2002, when the US economy was still absorbing the blow from the September 11 terrorist atrocities of the previous year.

But let's have a look at the evidence:

The chart below shows us how there have been 12 recessions in Canada dating back to World War 2. Just have a look at that chart. Consider that most investors bought near the market peaks and sold when the recessions became apparent.

Illustration 57: What's Really Important: Helping Clients Keep Perspective

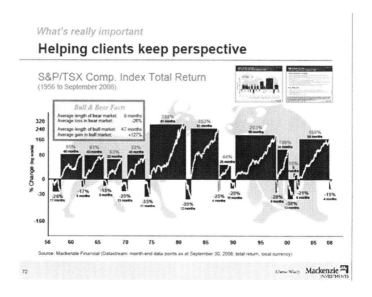

Consider what results would be if instead investors bought only during the recessions.

Now, this is really hard to do. As we have seen from the newspaper headlines during recessions, unemployment is high during recessions, people are worried about their job, the stock market analysts are forecasting worse is yet to come and making even more depressing predictions, and your investment advisor is often paralyzed. This is hardly a supportive atmosphere.

But let's look at the reporting of recessions. That is, let's look at when recessions are announced and what happened to the markets around such recessions.

Here is the data on three US recessions. (Canadian and US recessions happen pretty closely together.)

<u>Illustration 58: Three US Recessions:</u>

US Recessions					
Stock Market Peak	Date Recession Started	Date and Level Market Bottomed	Date Reccession Start Announced	Date Recession Ended	Date Recession End Announced
Jun-90	Jul-90	Oct-90	Apr-91	Mar-91	Dec-02
360.35	356.15	307.12 (-14.77%)	379.25	375.22	440.31 (+43.27%)
Aug-00	Mar-01	Oct-02	Nov-01	Nov-01	Jul-03
1485.46	1160.33	798.55 (-46.24)	1034.81	931.76	981.73 (+22.94%)
Oct-07	Dec-07	Mar-09	Dec-08	Jun-09	Sep-10
1561.8	1477.65	682.55 (-56.30%)	876.07	931.76	1146.67 (+68%)
Sources: NBER and Fundamentals of Managerial Economics by Mark Hirschey (Page 218, 2009 SouthWest Cengage)					
Average drop to bottom before announcement of start of recession: -39.10%					
Average rise from bottom before announcement of end of recession: +44.73%					

I am using data on the S&P 500 data. This index is based on the stock market prices of the largest 500 companies trading on the New York stock exchange.

The slide shows the date and level for the various key events before, during and after each recession.

In each case, the stock market fell *before* the recession started and well before the recession was announced.

In the 1990 recession, the start of the recession was announced *after* the recession was over.

During the recession of 2000, the start of the recession was announced in the month that it actually ended.

So, let's think about this.

The normal reflex action for most investors on hearing that we are in a recession is to become more conservative. That is, investors usually sell out of stocks and buy bonds or short term investments during recessions. Remember, after a recession is announced it is not unreasonable to believe that we are still in a recession until we are told otherwise. This was clearly wrong during these two recessions and data indicate that previous reporting on previous recessions was equally flawed.

Further, in all cases, the market rose *before* the end of the recession was announced. The amount of the rise from the market bottom is startling—43.27%, 22.94% and 68.00% respectfully.

A similar pattern occurred in 2008. That is, the market peaked in June 2007 and then fell drastically. And remember that the recession announcement was only made on December 31 of 2008, 12 months after the recession began and after the markets had fallen 80% of the total decline. As well, the market rose 68% from its bottom to the day that the end of the announcement was made.

This is compelling.

It appears that the announcement that we are in a recession is actually a good thing for investors. While it is not always a buy signal, history suggests that such announcements are usually made closer to the end of a recession rather than at the beginning of one.

Further, when you go back to the previous chapter on newspaper headlines, you can see that most economists and stock market prognosticators were not talking about a recession until after the stock market had fallen or discussing the end of a recession until after the market had recovered.

Let's take this one step further.

It is really the fear of a recession that drives most people out of the markets. Often the trigger that starts a discussion about a recession is some sort of a major calamity.

Below is a chart plotting out world calamities from 1940 to 1998 and showing the reaction to the event by the Dow Jones Industrial Average, one of the key measurements of the US market, over time. Remember that what happens to the US stock market usually is reflected directly in Canada's stock market.

Illustration 59: Crisis Events, DJIA Declines and
Subsequent Performance

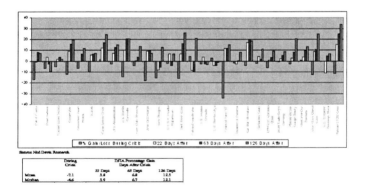

This chart plots the negative reaction at the crises event, then the market level 22 days later, 63 days later and 126 days after.

The average percentage return 126 days after the crises is a positive 12.5%. There were instances when the markets were still down but not catastrophically.

Now, I know that many people will say "Yes, but this time it's different" and point to September 11, 2001 as an example. However, the September 11, 2001 event was followed by the announcement of a new Iraqi war and within 126 days of the invasion of Iraq in April 2003, the markets were significantly higher.

Illustration 60: Reaction to Crisis Events

Reaction to Crisis Events

Dow Jones % Gain after Reaction

	Date Range % Gain/Loss	22 market days	63 market days	126 market days
MEAN	-7.1%	3.8%	6.8%	12.5%
MEDIAN	-4.6%	3.9%	6.7%	12.1%

So what we are seeing is that the announcement of a crisis—the headline—contributes to the selloff but effective government actions, including the cutting of interest rates and increasing money supply, stimulates a recovery.

So, should you be afraid of a recession?

One client said after seeing this presentation "Don't call me for new money to invest unless we are in one."

And remember when we talked about buy and hold as a strategy? A case could be made to start a buy and hold strategy during a recession and, if you are going to do that, ensure you have the intestinal fortitude to stick with it. But even then, with the increase in volatility we have seen in the last number of years, the ride could still be extremely upsetting.

Chapter 13

How to Read a Mutual Fund Ad:

(Hint—the smaller the letters the bigger the message)

We are going to talk about Mouse Speak versus Elephant Speak and chasing the winners versus chasing the losers.

Mutual Fund ads usually have a great proclamation such as "THIS FUND EARNED 30% PER YEAR FOR THE LAST FIVE YEARS" or more often, "THIS IS A FIVE STAR FUND".

The star systems are a means to rank mutual funds. The funds that have performed the best in the previous period are ranked five stars and the worst performers are ranked as one star.

In a great book called "The Age of Persuasion" author Terry O'Reilly talks about "Mouse Speak" or "asterisk speak". I like "Mouse Speak" for a number of reasons and I want to introduce the phrase "Elephant Speak" and you will see why in a moment.

Mouse Speak refers to the small words in an ad and in mutual fund ads they are next to the asterisk (hence the term, "asterisk speak").

The Elephant Speak is the headline proclamation. Now, understand that elephants are in fact afraid of mice. This was conclusively proven by Mythbusters on their TV program a few years ago.

The Mouse Speak on these ads read like this: "Blah blah blah . . . past performance is not indicative of the future . . ."

Here's the kicker: this is actually the most important part of the ad.

See, a series of studies has been done by Franklin Templeton and they found that this statement is really true—if you had to choose between buying the previous year's five star rated (winner) funds or the previous year's one star (losing) funds, where would you have made the most money?

The answer is that buying the funds that were one star funds gave a higher return at a lower risk than buying the five star funds. No wonder the elephant is afraid of the mouse.

So, when you read such an ad, it is not the time to buy. If you own the fund, odds are it is time to sell.

To add some additional ammo, please see the article below by one of the leading investment advisors in Canada. John J. De Goey has been an investment advisor for twenty years. He addressed this article to other investment advisors but I think that it is great advice for investors as well.

Additional point: People are more persistent than mutual funds

John J. De Goey / September 15, 2010

Tell me if you ever come across this statement before:

Commissions, trailing commissions, management fees and expenses all may be associated with mutual fund investments. Please read the prospectus before investing. Mutual funds are not guaranteed, their values change frequently and past performance may not be repeated.

This is, I'm sure you'll agree, the standard disclaimer found on mutual fund prospectuses and advertisements across the country. Everyone knows it. Everyone has seen it.

My question is: Why do so many people act as if it isn't true? If past performance cannot be relied upon for decision-making, why do so many people use that as their primary determinative consideration when choosing mutual funds?

If the disclaimer said "Reading tea leaves cannot be relied upon for making investment decisions" would you go to a client saying "Here are the products we have chosen for you based on our proprietary reading of your tea leaves?"

If it said "Reading chicken entrails is not a reliable way to go about making investment decisions" would you come to a client saying "This is the portfolio we have constructed for you by virtue of our proprietary, state-of-the-art reader of chicken entrails?"

If your answers are "No" then why would you even consider making recommendations based on past performance? Here's a simple exercise in logic. Let's not use past performance or entrails or tea leaves. Let's just call the thing in question "Process X". Here's the abbreviated statement:

This product is not guaranteed, its value changes frequently and reliance on Process X is not advised for decision-making. The point here is not whether Process X involves tea leaves, past performance or chicken entrails. No matter what the actual process is, it is unreliable: so for goodness sake, stop relying on it!

At issue here is the notion of persistence. Ever since Mark Carhart's groundbreaking study on the subject more than a generation ago, it has been widely recognized that the performance of mutual funds does not persist in any kind of a reliable fashion except that expensive, underperforming funds tend to continue to do so.

Ironically, even as past performance is a lousy predictor of future performance, current costs are an excellent predictor of future costs (translation: costs persist). There's also a well-established correlation between cost and performance. Please refer to just about anything written by John Bogle if you doubt me.

In offering advice to clients, I believe people should do what management thinker Rosemary Stewart suggests "focus on our sphere of influence rather than our sphere of concern. To whit: we may be concerned about performance, but we can't reliably control it. Meanwhile, we can control product costs (or at least select products based on costs that are highly likely to persist).

Management of anything (including your clients' portfolios) depends on how you work with the things you can control. If you can't control something, you can't manage it and no one can control mutual fund performance going forward. As such, I wonder why so many advisors persist in their product recommendations that are based primarily on past performance.

John J. De Goey, CFP is Vice President at <u>Burgeonvest Bick Securities Limited (BBSL).</u> The views expressed are not necessarily shared by BBSL.

Filed by John J. De Goey, *john.degoey@bbsl.ca*
Originally published on Advisor.ca

Chapter 14

How Your Investment Advisor Gets Paid Now and How Much Mutual Funds Cost

There is a tremendous amount of confusion about how advisors are paid and how investors are charged fees. Let's see if we can clear this up a bit.

There are four principal means by which an investment advisor gets paid.

The most basic form is salary and often this exists with "captive agents". Captive agents are employees who are hired to sell the company's own mutual funds. They are captive in the sense that they cannot sell competitors' funds, although they may have hybrids of other companies' funds. That is, the bank or insurance company may have a fund managed by one of the recent hot fund managers but privately labeled under their name. This was seen particularly during the high tech bubble of 1999-2000.

With captive agents, often there is a bonus structure built in if a sales quota is exceeded.

A second means of getting paid is through commissions. Here things can get a bit confusing.

There are captive agents who earn commissions by placing clients in the firm's own funds. Such commissions can be a "front end", which means that you are charged a fee to purchase the fund.

The commissions could also include a "trailer" where part of the embedded fee the mutual fund charges you annually is paid to the advisor.

The commissions could also be a "deferred sales charge" (DSC) aka "back end" arrangement. Most mutual funds in Canada are still sold this way. The commission is paid to the advisor by the mutual fund company and no acquisition fee is paid by you as long as you stay with the mutual fund company for a period of time, usually three to seven years. If the investor sells the funds that are still in the DSC schedule, they are charged a fee to get out. The advisor will also receive a reduced trailer during the time that the funds are held.

Most "non captive" or independent agents also get paid in the same manner.

There are also Investment Advisors who charge a flat fee for preparing a financial plan.

Finally, there are Investment Advisors who charge a flat fee or management fee for all transactions and services.

And of course, there are still individuals who work as traditional stockbrokers who charge a commission per transaction.

There is often confusion over mutual fund fees as well. In addition to any upfront or deferred mutual fund fees there is an annual fee. This fee is most often "embedded" meaning that it is not readily exposed. The return you see on your fund is after this fee has been charged.

I want to be very clear here—the fees are disclosed but done so in a document called a prospectus.

I joke that "prospectus" is "a Latin word meaning a complicated document written by accountants and lawyers for accountants and lawyers that no one reads." Disclosure is provided but the details are often hard to find and it can be quite confusing to root out the fees.

On a more serious note, one of the best explanations of mutual fund fees I have seen is provided by James Gauthier, an analyst at DundeeWealth. I have produced his report in full in Appendix A. It is called The True Cost of Fund Ownership.

What I found surprising about the report is that many investment advisors and industry experts believe that the full cost of owning a mutual fund is accurately represented by what is called the Management Expense Ratio (MER) of the fund. You can readily look up this fee for most mutual funds in Canada on various websites and in a company's prospectus. Usually it is expressed as a percentage of the fund and for 2009 Mr. Gauthier found that the average MER was 2.42% for Canadian equity (stock) funds.

However, there is an additional fee that many people are not aware of, even those in the industry. It is called the TER or Trading Expense Ratio. For many years I thought the cost of trading assets of the fund was part of the MER. It isn't and the only way to find it is to look at the financial statements of the fund itself.

This is what Mr. Gauthier did in his report, which is prepared annually. It turns out that the average TER for a Canadian equity fund in 2009 was 0.19%. This fee has to be added to the MER and that means that the total fee for the average Canadian equity fund in 2009 was 2.61%.

I am not aware of any other analyst preparing this type of report and I have little doubt that many industry participants still are not aware of the TER. You should be.

Chapter 15

How Your Investment Advisor Will be Paid in the Future and How Mutual Fund Fees Will be Disclosed In the Future

Hint: It will be different than now.

The industry is evolving and, according to Dan Sullivan, owner of Strategic Coach which is one of the premier coaching services in the world for investment advisors, changes to our industry tend to evolve in England, graduate to Australia and New Zealand and then migrate to the United States and eventually to Canada.

So, if we are to look to the future for your investment advisor and mutual funds we really just need to look to England now.

England announced in June of 2009 that commissions for financial advisors are banned as of 2012.

UK Bans Finance Advisers' Commission

By Matthew Vincent and Brooke Masters in London
Published: June 26 2009 03:00 | Last updated: June 26 2009 03:00

Financial advisers in the UK are to be banned from receiving commission for selling investment, pension and life insurance products from 2012, under radical rules announced by the Financial Services Authority, the industry regulator.

In a big review of the British financial services industry, the FSA set out measures to "ensure that commission-bias is removed from the system—and recommendations made by advisers are not influenced by product providers."

This headline was not covered much in my part of the world and I really do not think that many investment advisors in Canada really are aware of the significance of this announcement. This is a fundamental change in our industry with far reaching implications. It will change how mutual funds and insurance will be sold.

Surprisingly, it only took until November 2009 for Australia to announce that they too are considering such a ban. They want an upfront full and complete disclosure made as to how an advisor will charge his/her clients. Such fees cannot be embedded and it looks like the flat fee basis is going to become the standard for the industry.

An embedded fee is one that is built into the fund's return. That is, if your fund earned 10% and had an embedded fee of 2.61% (which by the way was the AVERAGE fee charged on an equity mutual fund in Canada in 2009). It means the fund actually earned 12.61%, subtracted the fee and gave you 10%.

Now 10% is still 10% regardless of whether the fee is disclosed or not but consider that the fund has to earn 2.61% for you to breakeven.

In the future, (we do not know when) you may have a statement from your mutual fund that shows how much money you started with, subtracts the fee and gives your net return. You can now see how dramatic this change is going to be to mutual funds and their salespeople.

Part of these changes relate to what is called the Client Relationship Model (CRM). The CRM is an attempt to address the potential conflict of interest that exists in our industry (and note the word "potential" because these conflicts are not confirmed). These potential conflicts have been highlighted because we profess to be professionals but our industry still operates on a sales mentality.

Try this test—ask your advisor who he/she reports to and then who that person reports to. Continue until you encounter the word "sales manager for . . ." It is always interesting to see how far one has to go to hit the word "sales manager" in an investment firm or bank.

As for mutual funds, the model in England will also require that funds more explicitly state how they charge so, again, no more embedded fees. All fees there will have to be shown as being deducted from your account.

The impact of these changes is profound. In England a large number of advisors have quit the industry because they felt that when they disclosed how much money they were making they were meeting resistance from their clients. Further they objected because, the argument goes, when you buy a dining room table the store does not tell you how much it made on the deal so why should the investor get to know how much the advisor was paid?

A similar situation is expected to arise in Canada. Take a look at your Investment Advisor. He/she may not be around in the years to come unless they are already moving their practice toward the Client Relationship Model or a close approximation.

And hope that your investment advisor is already in alignment with the CRM or is willing to adapt because your advisor is probably going to become even more valuable to you in the future.

Chapter 16

How to Choose a Financial Advisor

When I first came into this business in 1988 I noticed that a lot of the investment advisors, which were really stock brokers back then, came from the sales industry and included used car salesmen, paint store owners and others of similar ilk. The thought was that if you knew people, were sociably acceptable, and could sell then there was no difference between selling cars, paint or mutual funds.

This practice of hiring sales people continued up through the 1990's and there is a very interesting discussion in the book *A Colossal Failure of Common Sense* where Lawrence MacDonald, the trader who ended up in a senior position at Lehman, initially could not get a job on Wall Street because he had no sales experience. He talked about how he could not be hired until he had sufficient sales experience so he went to work with a food wholesaler and became the top pork salesman in New England. Yup—the broker had to sell pork chops before he was allowed to be an investment advisor. Only after he proved he could push pork could he get a job pushing stocks. There has to be a lesson in there somewhere.

Many of those sales people have thrived over the years and have done quite well for their clients but hiring practices have moved on since then. These days the emphasis is on a more formal education and, although it appears that the sales aspect is not emphasized as much initially, the fact is that if the new recruit does not meet their revenue quota they are either dismissed or their pay is cut drastically thereby encouraging them to leave the firm.

This quota is a pretty high hurdle so let's not fool ourselves by thinking that revenue generation is not a primary motivator for investment advisors. In Canada it is not uncommon for 7 out of 10 new recruits to not make it past their third year in the business because of the failure to meet this hurdle. In fact, the training program for new investment advisors is considered good if one gets 3 in 10 to survive beyond the third year. I worked at one branch of a national firm where none of the rookies ever made it over the hurdle during a five year period. This is pretty devastating on the rookie's ego as well as to their wallet.

One also has to wonder how any industry that spends as much time and money training new recruits finds it acceptable to have a 70% failure rate. Let's keep this in mind when you start interviewing prospective advisors.

Another source of confusion for investors looking to hire an advisor is the list of the various designations and titles that investment advisors go by. Titles really don't matter that much. As an investor, you are looking for someone to trust, and as a holder of a number of degrees, diplomas, designations and certifications and having met many more capable people with or without such letters behind their name, what this really means is that I know how to read books and retain enough information to be able to successfully write exams.

Don't get me wrong—the degrees and diplomas are an important factor but not as important as being able to connect with a client and communicate clearly with him/her. This ranks above all else.

If they do pass that test you will want someone who is licensed to meet your expectations. This is often spelled out by them in your initial conversations, an investment policy statement or an engagement letter. You will want to ensure the person is licensed for the investments you want to hold. The advisor should also be licensed to manage your portfolio on a discretionary basis (you have no input) or non-discretionary basis (you make the final decision, if it sounds reasonable). Further, you should know all the services they provide and the fees for such.

I came across the following article which, in light of the changes happening in our industry, is the best guide I have seen for interviewing a financial advisor. It is from the Financial Planning Standards Council of Canada.

Choosing a Planner

In your search for a competent financial planning professional, you need to be able to recognize who you can trust.

Financial planning is not regulated in most Canadian provinces. This means that anyone can call themselves a "financial planner". However, not everyone who refers to themselves as a planner is indeed qualified; many so-called financial planners are licensed to sell products but have no financial planning training or expertise.

In the absence of government regulation, consumers must ensure their planner is indeed trained, certified,

---

and held accountable in providing professional financial planning.

We offer you the following ten tips to prepare you and help you in your search for the right planner.

Choosing a Financial Planner: Ten Tips

1. Have an idea of your life goals: Determine your general financial goals and specific needs (insurance policy, estate planning, investments, education, etc.).
2. Be prepared: Do a bit of research to maximize your familiarity with financial planning strategies and terminology. Reading the business section of the newspaper or taking a look through some finance publications may be helpful.
3. Referrals are helpful, but not enough: Get referrals from advisors you trust, from colleagues and friends, but make sure you check into the planner's credentials. Check to see that person is in Good Standing with their professional body.
4. Look for competence: There are a variety of different degrees and designations in financial planning and investment services, and this can be confusing and overwhelming for many consumers.

   Although all the letters after the person's name can be impressive, some designations only require day or weekend courses to earn. Others, however, offer highly specialized knowledge in certain areas of a person's portfolio, or for a certain demographic. A Certified Financial Planner professional has met high standards of financial planning professionalism and abides by a Code of Ethics, which is strictly enforced by Financial Planners Standards Council.

5. Interview more than one planner: Ask each person to outline their education, experience and specialties, the size and duration of their practices, how often they communicate with clients, and whether assistants handle client matters. You need to make sure that you feel comfortable discussing your finances with the individual you select, as this is a personal subject.

6. Check the planner's background: call their professional associations to check on their complaint or disciplinary record. You can call FPSC to see if they are a CFP® professional in good standing or check them out online using the In Good Standing tool.

7. Ask for references: Find out if the financial planner works with any other professionals such as accountants, insurance agents or legal advisors. After the meeting, request references from these individuals.

8. Know what to expect: Ask for a registration or disclosure document detailing method of compensation, conflicts of interest, business affiliations and personal qualifications.

9. Get it in writing: Insist on a written letter outlining the specific terms of the engagement. Never agree to sign anything you are not clear about. Verbal promises should be considered a red flag. Ensure that the planner\'s compensation is thoroughly explained and documented—make sure you understand how the planner is being paid. Insist on obtaining written notification of any changes to compensation structure during your relationship.

10. Re-assess the relationship regularly: Financial planning relationships are quite often long-term. Review your relationship on a regular basis, making sure your planner understands your needs as they change and develop over time. Make appropriate

alternations to your plan, as you needs evolve and your financial situation changes. It's important for you to stay engaged with the process. Open and read all statements; ask your planner for clarification if you don't understand something.

10 Questions to Ask Your Planner

You may be seeking help from a financial planner for a number of reasons: planning for retirement, finding the best way to finance a new home, saving for children's education or simply to get help putting finances in order. Whatever your needs, working with a financial planner can be a helpful step in securing your financial future.

Finding the right planner is extremely important because your choice will almost certainly affect your financial future. These questions will help you interview and evaluate several financial planners to find a competent, qualified professional with whom you feel comfortable and whose business style suits your financial needs.

Think of interviewing a potential planner as similar to interviewing a person who is applying for a job you've posted. In a way, they are—they want to be your personal money manager! And you need to ask the right questions to see if this person is ethical and competent to handle the responsibility of managing your financial future.

Don't be afraid to ask these and any other questions you feel need a full and open answer. Any professional will welcome them.

1. What are your qualifications?
2. What experience do you have?
3. What services do you offer?

4. <u>What is your approach to financial planning?</u>
5. <u>Will you be the only person working with me?</u>
6. <u>How will I pay for your services?</u>
7. <u>How much do you typically charge?</u>
8. <u>Could anyone besides me benefit from your recommendations?</u>
9. <u>Are you regulated by any organization?</u>
10. <u>Can I have it in writing?</u>

1. What are your qualifications?

Financial planning is a detailed, comprehensive process. It requires hands-on experience and a strong technical understanding of topics such as personal tax planning, insurance, investments, retirement planning and estate planning—and how a recommendation in one area can affect the others.

Ask the planner what her qualifications are to offer financial advice and if, in fact, she is a qualified planner. Ask what training she has successfully completed. Ask what steps she takes to keep up with changes and developments in the financial planning field and the financial services industry at large.

Ask whether she holds any professional credentials or designations. Certified Financial Planner certification, which is recognized internationally as the mark of the competent, ethical, professional financial planner, is held by almost 17,500 people across Canada.

2. What experience do you have?

Experience is an important consideration in choosing any professional. Ask how long the planner has been in practice, the number and types of firms with which he has been associated, and how his work experience relates to his current practice. Inquire about what experience the planner has in dealing with people in similar situations to yours and whether he has any specialized training. Choose a financial planner who has at least two years experience counseling individuals on their financial needs.

3. What services do you offer?

The services a financial planner offers will vary and depend on her credentials, registration, areas of expertise and the organization for which she works. Some planners offer financial planning advice on a range of topics but do not sell financial products. Others may provide advice only in specific areas such as estate planning or taxation. Those who sell financial products such as insurance, stocks, bonds and mutual funds, or who give investment advice, must be registered with provincial regulatory authorities and may have specialized designations in these areas of expertise.

4. What is your approach to financial planning?

The types of services a financial planner will provide vary from organization to organization. Some planners prefer to develop detailed financial plans encompassing all of a client's financial goals. Others choose to work in specific areas such as taxation, estate planning, insurance and investments. Ask whether the individual deals only with clients with specific net worth and income levels, and whether the planner will help you implement the plan she develops or refer you to others who will do so.

5. Will you be the only person working with me?

It is quite common for a financial planner to work with others in his organization to develop and implement financial planning recommendations. Financial planners often work with other professionals, like lawyers and accountants. You may want to meet everyone who will be working with you.

6. How will I pay for your services?

Your planner should disclose in writing how she will be paid for the services she will provide. Planners can be paid in several ways:

Commission: The planner is compensated if you purchase financial products to implement a financial planning recommendation. In some cases, the commission is paid by the suppliers of financial products such as an insurance company. In other cases, you pay the commission, for example, if you buy shares of a publicly traded company. Commissions are usually a percentage of the amount you invest in a product.

Salary: The company for which the planner works pays the planner a salary. The planner's employer may get its revenues from fees paid by clients such as yourself or in commissions paid by clients making a purchase, or by the suppliers of financial products.

Fee-for-service: Planners paid on a fee-for-service basis may charge an hourly rate, set a flat rate for a specific service or be paid a fee based on a percentage of assets or income. In some cases, compensation would be a mix of fee and commission. You should also ask if the planner or organization receives any benefit other than commission, such as advertising and promotion subsidies, from suppliers of financial products.

7. How much do you typically charge?

Although the amount you pay the planner depends on your particular needs, the financial planner should be able to provide you with an estimate of possible costs based on the work to be performed. Such costs would include the planner's hourly rates or flat fees, or the percentage he would receive as commission on products you may purchase as part of the financial planning recommendations.

8. Could anyone besides me benefit from your recommendations?

Ask the planner to provide you with a description of her conflicts of interest in writing, for instance, any business relationship with the companies or ownership interest in any company that supplies financial products sold by the planner and the planner's employer.

9. Are you regulated by any organization?

Financial planners who sell financial products such as securities and insurance or who provide investment advice are regulated by provincial regulatory authorities and may also subscribe to a code of ethics through a professional association. Individuals in the accounting and legal professions are usually members of professional bodies that govern their fields. Planners who hold CFP® certification are subject to disciplinary proceedings of Financial Planners Standards Council, the body that enforces that CFP Code of Ethics.

It's a fair question to ask if he has ever been the subject of disciplinary action by any regulatory body or industry association. You can verify the answer by contacting the relevant organization; some organizations have a searchable function on their websites, such as the Check a CFP Professional tool on this website.

Ask the financial planner whether he subscribes to a professional code of ethics such as the Certified Financial Planner Code of Ethics.

10. Can I have it in writing?

Ask the planner to provide you with a written agreement that details the services that will be provided. Keep this document in a secure place, for future reference.

Chapter 17

Solution One: Becoming a Contrarian

So now that you know the problems related to investor behaviour, advisor behaviour, the importance of acting opposite to the market sentiment, how to really read a newspaper, how to operate in a sales oriented environment, and seeing how limited Modern Portfolio Theory is, how do you make investment decisions?

There are three solutions that I know of.

The first relates to the lessons that you have learned so far.

I hope that this far in the book you are better armed than you were before reading this book. So if nothing changes except that you are now better aware of those aspects of investing discussed so far then you have increased your chances of prospering.

Solution One is therefore to become a Contrarian. If you become a Contrarian you have come over to my side of the force. As a Contrarian you question modern portfolio theory and generally all methods of investing. You question the trend following and the conclusions drawn by most analysts. You read a newspaper different than how most readers do, looking at miserable headlines as an opportunity to buy and optimistic headlines as a clue as to when to sell.

This is actually a lot harder than it sounds. There are few specific tools that mark a Contrarian although Ned Davis does provide a chapter on indicators of crowd psychology in *The Triumph of Contrarian Investing* (McGraw Hill, 2004).

Being a Contrarian is really a change in attitude.

If you can make this conversion in attitude, continue on with the tools and investment advisor you have always had but, now that you are better prepared to interpret market information differently, prepare for combat. Often you will have a hard time maintaining a position opposite to the consensus opinion and when you are wrong, which will happen because this method tends to be ahead of the curve, hold your positions until the market changes or new information causes you to change your mind.

Always keep in mind that you can be perfectly correct in your assessment that the market is underpriced or overpriced and this irrational condition can continue to prevail. For example, there is little question that high tech and internet stocks were overvalued for quite a while during the years 1999 and 2000 but that overvaluation prevailed for a long time. Similarly, the US real estate market was overvalued for several years up to 2009.

Adopting a Contrarian approach is such a difficult solution because, as economist John Maynard Keynes put it "The market can stay irrational longer than you can stay solvent."

Chapter 18

Solution Two:
Fixing Modern Portfolio Theory

If we take the best parts of Modern Portfolio Theory and modify it we may be able to employ a less difficult to maintain solution. Let's break down the problems into manageable pieces.

1) The Failure of Modern Portfolio Theory

As discussed in Chapter 9, one of the key problems in our industry relates to the overall performance of equity managers in general and we illustrated this with the SPIVA study.

Lets's call this the **Performance and Prediction Problem**.

It is often stated that past performance is not an indicator of future performance but investors intuitively believe that past performance must matter somewhat. Further, salesmen (and women) in our industry often attract customers by advertising "5 star" funds and "top performing funds" as part of their sales programs. This form of marketing reinforces the misconception of predictability, raises expectations and increases the subsequent disappointment when the returns are not as advertised.

The SPIVA report confirms that past performance is not a predictor of future performance of a traditional mutual fund manager. In fact, returns of traditional mutual fund managers are not sufficiently predictable to be relied upon.

2) We also discussed how Canadian Large Cap Equity managers often tend to inadvertently replicate the S&P/TSX Composite index. This relates to the hollowing out of the Toronto Stock Exchange and that as long as mutual fund and pension fund managers do not deviate too much from the index they can hold on to their jobs. As long as they are not worse than average, which could arise if they took on a position different from the index, they are safe. And because that limits them to investing in the largest 44 stocks because they are so big, it reinforces the replication of the index. Stepping out of "normal" is risky to these managers personal career.

Let's call this the **Liquidity Risk and Personal Promotion Problem**.

3) There is another element contributing to such high correlation between managers and that is the lack of a sell discipline. Modern Portfolio Theory advocates that no investment manager can time the market and therefore, an investment manager should keep the client fully invested at all times. We call this the **Sell Discipline Problem**.

We have to recognize these problems and address them in the following manner:

1) **Performance and Prediction Solution**: Rather than attempt to find the 3% to 9% of managers that may beat the index in the next five years what if we invest in the index itself by purchasing an index based exchange traded fund (ETF). This solution means that investors' accounts will have a higher likelihood of outperforming the vast majority of traditional mutual fund managers.

As shown in the SPIVA study, active investment methodologies have in the past been the Achilles Heel of our business, requiring considerable time and more often than not yielding poorer returns than investing in the indices directly. The use of index ETFs also generates another clear benefit:

Simplicity.

Through the use of ETFs one can achieve proper diversification without necessarily owning a large number of positions. This has the advantage of being easier to track and allows you to know the details of each position more intimately.

2) **Liquidity Risk and Personal Promotion Solution:** Because of the highly liquid nature of the index ETFs you are not limited to selling individual stocks or bonds to other institutional investors when you want to get out.

3) **Sell Discipline Solution:** This, above all else, is a key part to this strategy. I don't think we can blindly believe in Modern Portfolio Theory or, by implication, that diversification alone can protect clients' capital in the event of a dramatic market decline.

This means that the Buy and Hold strategy is no longer valid. It appears that we have re-entered a stock market pattern where markets will not always rise but where markets will move in increasingly wider swings where we will have higher new highs followed by larger corrections.

This increase in volatility has occurred for a number of reasons, but most notably, because of the ability of individual investors to move in and out of the markets easily, combined with instant reporting of worldwide news that tends to enhance investor fear and market pessimism.

It is recommended that a sell discipline be implemented whereby, once a level of profit has been achieved, money be taken off the table. That is, as markets rise the percentage of the account allocated to short term bonds and cash would rise.

To be clear here—evidence is strong that if you purchase the index ETFs and **do not** impose a sell discipline solution that there is a high probability of outperforming the vast majority of fund managers. This is a passive investment approach. If a sell discipline is added after a profit level has been obtained the risk to the investor is decreased and the probability of positive returns over time is increased.

Although this seems like a relatively simple strategy it is very powerful and very difficult to put into practice. It relies on tactical asset allocation, technical analysis, monitoring the media and market sentiment readings. Really, it relies on judgment, which cannot be easily quantified.

It should be noted that under this solution investors should be willing to make reasonable returns at relatively lower risk rather than attempt to make very high returns at higher risk. This means that they should be willing to leave money on the table rather than engage in the last part of the run up in a market.

This combination of the use of Index ETF's, employing the latest in research, the use of a sell strategy, and the use of a risk reduction methodology makes for an interesting solution.

This is a lot of work, either for you or for your advisor and, although it will not guarantee success, it does improve your odds dramatically.

Failing that there is one more potential solution. This one has been around a long time—well before Modern Portfolio Theory was even imagined.

Chapter 19

Solution Three:The Value Manager and the Concentrated Portfolio

This solution is often glossed over and when reviewed is often still not presented from the proper viewpoint.

Let me put it like this: another alternative to Modern Portfolio Theory is called Value Investing and it involves using a concentrated portfolio of stocks that one buys and holds for a long period of time.

This methodology is based on a book called *Security Analysis* published in 1934 by Benjamin Graham. His best known follower is Warren Buffett who was tutored and employed by Mr. Graham for many years.

Based on the principles outlined in the book and no doubt with considerable coaching from Mr. Graham himself, Mr. Buffett took a relatively small amount of money, invested it in the stock market and turned it into a fortune significantly large enough that he now ranks as being one of the wealthiest people in history.

There are many followers of this methodology in Canada and some of the best known value managers include Michael Lee Chin, Ned Goodman and Gerry Coleman.

Michael Lee Chin borrowed $500,000 in 1983 and invested it in one stock, Mackenzie Financial Corporation. After four years the stock appreciated seven fold and Michael used the profits to make his first acquisition, a small investment firm called AIC Limited. At the time AIC Limited's assets under management were merely $800,000. Within 20 years, AIC Limited grew from less than $1 million to more than $15 billion at its business peak, putting Michael on the Forbes Billionaire list.

Ned Goodman was appointed president of Dynamic funds in 1968 and bought out the fund family from Beutel Goodman and Co in 1987. He used that as a basis to build DundeeWealth, one of Canada's most successful investment houses, and built his personal fortune using the same methodology.

Gerry Coleman manages one of the largest mutual funds in Canada for CI Investments. He was named Money Manager of the Decade by the *Globe and Mail* in 2010.

There have been many books written on this methodology since Benjamin Graham wrote his and most focus on "the Warren Buffett Way" or on "Buy, Hold and Prosper" which Michael Lee Chin espouses which advocates how the average individual can make money like the big guys using this Security Analysis approach.

Value Investing, in its most simple form, involves buying excellent companies that are undervalued and holding them until they are overvalued or other, better companies are more undervalued. There's your buy and sell strategy—sounds logical and straightforward, doesn't it?

Many mutual funds in Canada and around the world claim to follow exactly this process and often go by the label "value funds" or that the manager is a "value manager". For example, Gerry Coleman of CI Investments clearly states that he is a value manager even though the full name of the huge balanced fund he is managing is Harbour Growth & Income Fund.

Confusing, isn't it?

Here is what is missing from most explanations.

In this book we have seen how many investors buy at the wrong time and sell at the wrong time.

Remember the discussion about recessions? Remember how most investors sell when they hear of a recession or when their investment falls in value?

Think about buying only recession proof companies and buying them when everyone else is selling them. In this way you become an owner of great companies—companies that will survive the recession, not just this one but all recessions, and actually prosper because their competition goes bankrupt during the recession but they survive. Then you become not a speculator in companies you know nothing about, not a gambler, not a casino player—but an owner in the truest sense of the word.

Now, when the markets fall you have a better appreciation of the companies you own. You are less inclined to sell and may actually buy more when a company's stock price falls.

Sound familiar?

This is the essence of a Value Manager.

But most investors cannot do this. Most do not research the companies they own. Most think that mutual funds are "things that have gone up in the last five years so they are always going to go up". They do not understand their investments and often do not know the companies they have put their money into. They just think they have bought a "mutual fund".

This is sacrilege. They bought by looking backwards. They thought that the next five years would look like the last five years and had no understanding about how markets work.

They bought on the basis of the wrong decision rule—the historical return—it went up in the last five years—and consequently will sell on the basis of that same decision rule if the fund goes down.

The true Value Manager methodology changes the decision rule. Under this methodology you do not buy stock—you buy great businesses. You just happen to use the stock market to buy it from less knowledgeable investors who sell the company's shares to you because they do not know as much about the businesses as you do. Or, using a mutual fund, you partner with a manager who knows how to find and buy such great businesses at great prices.

Investing in this manner was around before Modern Portfolio Theory was formulated and for many years people like Ned Goodman, Michael Lee Chin, and Warren Buffett employed it and they have actually beaten the underlying indices pretty consistently, although more so before 1998.

Since 1998, Warren Buffett's results continue to be exceptionally strong but Warren Buffett has a number of key advantages over other value manager practitioners.

One of the key advantages that Warren Buffett has is the structure of his investments. Let me explain by example.

Let's go back to 1998 with Michael Lee Chin's funds under the banner of the mutual fund company he owned, AIC Ltd.

Michael Lee Chin was managing AIC Advantage Fund and his philosophy led him to invest in Canadian banks and mutual fund companies (that is, the companies that put together and managed the mutual funds) in that fund.

The growth in these stocks from 1992 to early 1998 had been truly phenomenal. Then, to top it off, the Canadian banks announced that they were going to pair off and merge to form even stronger and more profitable businesses so that brought the bank stocks up to even higher levels.

This great call on the financial sector earned spectacular returns for Michael Lee Chin's fund over that period and he beat the returns of the Toronto Stock Market index by a country mile.

In our business as discussed earlier, we commonly receive phone calls from mutual fund representatives where they try to impress the investment advisors with how smart their fund managers are and see if we will start selling their funds. These people are referred to in our industry as "wholesalers".

I distinctly remember the AIC wholesaler for Eastern Canada calling me early in 1998 and he made the following statement:

"Larry, you are one of the few advisors in the province of Newfoundland and Labrador not selling our flagship fund. How come?"

I was in my tenth year in the business and had learned a few things by then and was surrounded by some very bright people in the industry. One practice I had adopted began in 1993 when I would ask mutual fund wholesalers for a copy of their recommendations when we met and I would file them and bring those recommendations to a meeting with them one year later.

In most cases, the recommendation was to buy the hot fund of the day and, usually, the hot fund peaked shortly after so the track record of many of these wholesalers was pretty poor. One chap had five different hot funds crash over a five year period.

I did learn though, that if I asked which fund the wholesaler was most embarrassed about, which is the one that has dropped the most, I left with some interesting possibilities. After all, who could be interested in a fund that dropped 40% from the previous year? Often the one that had dropped the most was the one that had been the hot fund the previous year.

So, along comes this AIC wholesaler with "Why are you not buying the best fund in Canada?"

My answer was that I could not buy a fund that was at its all time high.

He correctly pointed out that it had been going through all time highs just about every day for two years now.

I asked him if he was getting a lot of new money pouring into the fund. He confirmed that indeed, a lot of new money was coming into the fund. In fairness, here was a fund that had delivered as promised. It had provided returns that had beat the index on a consistent basis for a considerable period of time.

I said "Someday the fund will stumble. Please call me then." I was not making a forecast and it was blind luck that what I hoped would happen did.

Sure enough, in April 1998 the Federal Minister of Finance at the time, Mr. Paul Martin, announced that the Canadian banks could not merge and down came the bank stocks. To add to the misery, the Asian Currency crises and the bankruptcy of Russia contributed to a Toronto Stock Exchange market decline of 38% by September 1998. Most Canadian bank stocks were down by 50% and one was down by over 60%.

AIC Advantage, like many other value funds, fell dramatically.

Then two things happened.

First, I called the AIC wholesaler and asked if we could do a client event on AIC Advantage Fund. I think he was very pleasantly surprised and this began a long friendship that continues to this day.

Second, I asked him if investors were taking money out of the fund.

The answer was a resounding "Yes" and "Yes", which explained his surprise at my offer to do a client event to encourage clients to put money into the AIC Advantage Fund.

But this second question turned out to be the more important of the two and explains a lot about why the concentrated portfolio method that Warren Buffett employs, and Ned Goodman's fundamental security analysis process results in, and as Michael Lee Chin states with his "Buy, Hold and Prosper" slogan causes him to move toward, is so very difficult to put into practice.

Think about the last question from the fund manager's position:

Premise: value managers will buy when a company is undervalued.

Q: When is a company most undervalued?

A: When there is a panic and good companies are sold down in price for the wrong reason.

Q: When is the single best time for investors to give cash to a value manager?

A: When there is panic in the air.

Q: What did investors do in the panic of September, 1998 after the market had fallen 38% in six months? Remember their decision rule to buy the fund was "It had gone up." So their sell decision rule was to sell if "It went down." They had no idea about what they were investing in and had relied on a false rule.

A: They took money from all the value managers.

So, money came out of Michael Lee Chin's and Ned Goodman's funds and many other value managers.

And how did the money come out?

Well the value managers had to sell some of the companies they held, which they had bought at higher prices, to provide cash to those investors who wanted out of the fund.

So, if they bought shares of companies that were undervalued at higher prices than they were trading for in September of

1998, logically these companies were even more undervalued by the time of the September 1998 panic, meaning these managers were selling at the worst possible time.

But they had no choice—investors made the decision to sell. They forced the manager's hand. They said "given me my money" and the manager had to sell.

Except for Warren Buffett.

See, he has a different structure. He does not have an "open ended mutual fund" which is the technical term for the type of fund that most Canadians are investing in.

He has an investment company trading on the stock exchange and this has provided him with a key advantage over traditional mutual fund managers.

That advantage, which AIC and many other value managers do not have, is that if you want to get your money out of Warren Buffett's company, Berkshire Hathaway, you sell the shares of Berkshire Hathaway, in the open market on the New York Stock Exchange.

How does that affect Warren's decision when to invest in the market?

It doesn't.

He is the decider of when or what to buy or sell. The investor in his company is not the person forcing Warren to buy or sell. He makes that decision. The investor just decides to stay with him or go elsewhere by buying or selling shares in his company.

He does not have to sell the companies he owns in Berkshire Hathaway to send money to the investor.

See, if you sell units of a regular "open ended" equity mutual fund in Canada the manager must sell stocks in the fund to raise cash to send to you, the client. In September 1998 that meant selling at the worst possible time.

Buffett's structure meant he did not face this pressure and was free to buy when others were selling and this has proved to be a huge advantage, not only in 1998, but whenever the market has plunged.

Probably the best example for Buffett was in 1973. Back then the nation of Israel and their Arab neighbours got into a war and, to put pressure on the Western Powers who were supporting Israel, the Arab oil countries and their allies tripled the price of oil overnight and cut supplies. The stocks on the New York Stock Exchange, including shares of the company, Washington Post, plunged.

At that time, Warren Buffett, not worried about having to sell to fund redemptions, invested $11 million in shares of the Washington Post.

Now fast forward to December 2008. Those shares were valued at $679 million and that was after the stock market crash of 2008.

Understand this please—Warren Buffett did not make a special deal with the Washington Post. Any of us could have put $11,000 dollars into shares of the Post and seen them soar to $679,000 by December 31, 2008 (they were actually worth over a million in 2007) so he had no special deal.

His wisdom was there but the structure was too.

You have to have the wisdom to buy but when your investors are asking for cash back, a value manager has no choice and cannot act in the best interest of their client investors. The Warren Buffett way cannot be done without the proper structure.

I think we can all see that "closed end funds" of the type that Warren Buffett is using and ETF's will be the leading structures in the future. Their advantages are clear. They allow a value manager to do his/her job when they best can.

When you can find those closed ended funds run by a competent value manager or value index ETF's, you have another alternative to those funds using Modern Portfolio Theory.

In the meantime, you can use the traditional open ended value manager funds, if you can buy them or stay with them when everyone else is panicking.

Chapter 20

How to Deal with Inheriting Money, Selling a Business or Winning a Lottery

The first step after this has happened is to do one thing above all else:

Do nothing.

Place the money in the most secure investment you can find, either a Treasury Bill or a Money Market Fund, and go find a beach, a cabin, or a cruise but recognize that the change that takes place when you receive money is equal to mourning a loss.

I know that sounds strange but it is true.

We have had clients win millions in lotteries and curse the day they did. We have had clients sell their business and become multimillionaires but rue the day they did.

The point is that such a change in life is a loss, even though you won't recognize it for some time.

The getaway allows the mind to focus and the body to relax. It is only when we step away from the bustle of life that we can see our priorities.

You can come back to your regular life when you feel you can finish the following statement:

"Here is what I would like to happen in my life in the next three years: . . ."

Otherwise, stay on the beach, in the cabin or on the cruise.

Some years ago, I was asked a question by a business owner. He said, "have you ever watched a dog chase a bus and snap at the tires? Did you ever wonder what would happen if the dog actually caught the bus and bit his teeth into the tire? What would the dog do?"

In his case, he explained how he had reacted like a dog after a bus in the past and reached for and was awarded a massive contract that he could not complete in the end. He had planned to get the contract, but he had not planned what to do afterwards, in the same way that the dog thought he knew how to catch the bus but would have no idea what to do once he caught the bus.

A similar sort of thinking pervades when it comes to receiving large sums of money in one form or another, either through receiving an inheritance, the sale of your business or winning a lottery.

Let's first focus on lotto winners.

There's an old joke about winning the lotto where one spouse calls the other and says "pack your things, I've checked the tickets, and we won the lotto!" To which the other spouse replies "Should I pack for the sunny south or the snowy north?" The reply comes back from the spouse holding the winning ticket: "I don't care what you pack as long as you're out of the house when I get home."

This sounds like a pretty crude joke, but unfortunately it's made cruder by the fact that it's often true. The winning of a lotto is the same as catching a bus; that is, people say here's what I think I'm going to do, but they don't realize that there are dramatic ramifications that arise afterwards. In many cases, families split up.

But this holds true not just for lotto winners. It also holds true for people selling their business or receiving an inheritance. In each case there is often a change in perspective by the family members.

Prior to selling a family business, it is not unusual for the family to feel that it is "them against the world," that they're working and competing as a family unit, holding the business together and working hard as a family. They share common interests, beliefs and values.

When the business is sold, particularly if all of the members of the family are aware of the proceeds, there often is a conflict as to how the distribution should be handled.

As well, business owners often feel very much in control because they are the ones who make all the business decisions.

In addition to the mechanics within the family; that is, in addition to the relationships within the family coming under strain, there's a change in the way that business owners have to look at their investments.

There are two points here. First, as a general statement, business owners make more money in their business than they will in the stock or bond market. This to a degree reflects the real risk of a single individual private business versus that of a broad-based market, but the perception is that the family business is less risky than investing in the overall market. Regardless of whether or not that is true, and it is, the perception that an individual can make money in a private business is a sound statement.

It is not unrealistic for an individual in their private business to make an internal rate of return of 20 to 30% over a significant period of time. This is what makes them wealthy.

After selling a business, however, they should be looking at the proceeds of sale as being after-risk money. After-risk money means that you've already put your sweat equity into it and tolerated significant risk. As a consequence, the money that is left over should be invested at a much lower risk.

It is not unusual for business owners to become frustrated with their after-business sale returns because they are used to having more control and they are used to earning higher rates of return than stocks and bonds traditionally deliver.

One other factor that has to be taken into account is the actual day of valuation on one's business. It is not unusual to have a business valued a number of times during one's career. As a business owner you may have valued when you first start up in order to set up an insurance policy to cover debts; part-way through the life of the business you may have it re-valued again for estate planning purposes; and then the day of sale would be the third time that the business would be valued. Over a 30-year career you may end up having the business valued as little as three times. However, when one begins to invest in the stock market, the value of the person's net worth becomes valued on a daily basis and these days, with technology, it can be valued on an hourly basis.

Consequently, one of the worries that one has to contend with in transitioning from having your net worth valued as your family business versus your net worth being valued as the value of your investment portfolio, relates to what I'll call financial energy requirements.

The financial energy requirements come from the fact that we have cognitive dissonance (conflicting ideas). Cognitive dissonance means that once an individual makes an investment they will often go back and question that investment, particularly if there's new information that becomes available after the investment decision has been made.

Another way to look at it is that based on the best information available at the time an individual will make an investment. Subsequent information will then become available that causes that individual to question their investment. Such subsequent information can be knowledge, things that the investor has learned, or a change in economics or business news.

Investors often feel drained after making investment decisions. For them to go back and question again the same investment decisions time and again requires further mental energy to do so. So as a consequence when an individual then makes an investment decision and sees their investment fall in value and then has to make another decision whether to stay in or reinvest more, they can often become exhausted and frustrated with the investment process.

This relates to a business owner because again we have the business owner only valuing their business three times over a 30-year period, whereas the investments they make after selling their business into the stock and bond markets are valued on a daily basis.

They were aware that although there was no ticker on the outside of their business building as they went to work every day; in truth their business was fluctuating. No one drew their attention to this because it wasn't an automatic daily updating of the value of their business, it never became something that they focused on or spent time and energy on. This actually allowed them to make the long-term investment decisions that they needed to make.

However, because of the daily pricing of their investments after selling the business, they start to question and start to spend mental energy trying to decide whether to stay in their investments or move out.

If you have won a significant amount of money, I wish you better luck in the future. Money will be no problem but other aspects of your life will suffer unless you take time to do the proper planning. We've had a number of lottery winners as clients over the years and the most successful ones have been ones who follow a number of steps. Unfortunately, there are fewer successful ones than unsuccessful.

The first recommendation to lotto winners is to do nothing.

There are several reasons for doing nothing.

The single most important reason is that winning a large amount of money can change all of your personal and business relationships and often those changes are not in a favourable manner. Money can act on your relationships like gasoline on a fire. It can quickly raise expectations about you by others, affect judgment and priorities, and lead to a lot of disappointment. Over the years we have had a number of lottery winners tell us they wish they had never won the money because of the damage done to relationships with previously close friends and families.

There is the very public case of Mr. Jack Whittaker in the United States who won $113 million in 2002. You think that much money would buy at least some happiness but within two years, his life was a mess beyond belief and he is only one example of many. If you would like to know more, just search "unhappy lotto winners" on your computer.

Of course, this does not happen in all cases. We have had other lotto winners who quite happily received their winnings and continued on with their lives almost as if the lottery had never happened.

To a large extent, the change is driven by the winners themselves and has its roots in how they react to the impact of the winnings. Most winners react with great excitement because, of course, all of their money problems have been solved, they are suddenly incredibly popular with everyone and they have become a local celebrity that everyone suddenly envies, and defers to. This is an intoxicating experience and it is understandable how one could just go with the flow and enjoy it to the point of being overwhelmed. Often grand gifts are granted and great promises made to family and friends without thinking of how this will change relationships around you.

It is surprising how many relatives one suddenly becomes aware of, how many friends and associates that may appear on the scene. There is an amount of pressure that will be applied as everyone has opinions and suggestions as to how the money should be distributed and where it should be invested. Also, winning the lottery attracts some of the greatest investment salesmen in the business and one must be aware of that.

This is not a recommendation to not share but it is a recommendation to proceed quietly, slowly and most importantly, privately in distribution of your largesse and this is best done starting out by doing nothing.

Now, it is very hard to do nothing.

It is in the lottery corporation's interest that as much publicity as possible be gleaned from your winnings and usually a press conference and photo opportunity is provided to the media. Also, the name and address of the person who wins the lotto must be made known. These two steps make it difficult to resist moving on to a grandiose party and then on to a buying and gifting spree.

It is actually in the winner's best interest to make themselves as least well known as possible. It is fully understandable that the lotto winner must be named. However, whether the winner is treated to the full publicity experience or not is entirely up to the lotto winner themselves. To be clear, the winner must provide a photo opportunity, but who says it has to be right away?

It has been recommended by one of our lotto winners that the winner should claim the prize but not accept the money right away. That is, the ticket should be duly and properly recorded as being a winner, the person's name will be published but the press conference and photo opportunity postponed. It is then recommended that the winner get away from their community for an extended period of time. I would recommend that this be at least a six-month period. This will give the winner the opportunity to adjust to their dramatic new lifestyle.

Picking up the cheque after six months will not garner the news coverage it would have if the conference had been held days after the winning. Six months later it is old news and may solicit no interest by the various news agencies.

It is also recommended that the individual winners change all their telephone numbers and give their new phone numbers only to those individuals that they have selected as being close and personal.

They should also park their money in the single most secure investment they possibly can, most likely government of Canada bonds, until such time as they can determine what to do with their winnings. I met one lottery winner who invested $10 million within days of receiving the cheque. She then parked herself in front of the TV to watch the business news and saw her money move up and down more in one day than she had made in a year. She ended up with migraines.

In writing this I am reminded of one of my favourite pieces of writing. It is called the *Desiderata* and was copyrighted by Max Erhmann in 1927.

The first two sections out of the piece seem most appropriate for lotto winners:

Go placidly amid the noise and haste, and remember what peace there may be in silence.

As far as possible, without surrender, be on good terms with all persons. Speak your truth quietly and clearly; and listen to others, even to the dull and the ignorant, they too have their story. Avoid loud and aggressive persons, they are vexations to the spirit.

Regardless of whether one inherits money, wins it by a lotto or wins it by sale of a business, primary consideration should be given to how the children will be affected. Often in our society a measure of a person is dependent on how much money that they have. But really the measure of a person is not how high one stands at one point in time in terms of wealth. It is better measured from where a person started in their economic life, how many times that person has been knocked down economically and stood back up again and where they stand today. Unfortunately, having money given to you diminishes its value. Sweating over a dollar increases the worth of that dollar. Winning a lotto, selling a business or receiving an inheritance can often cause an individual's personal worth to be diminished and this will have ramifications down the road. There are clear examples of that in our society. On the world stage, there are individuals such as the heiress of a hotel chain who is famous for being famous but I would be embarrassed to call her a child of mine. We wish for our children to be profitable and beneficial contributors to society and in the cases of certain wealthy celebrities we can see examples of children who have gone awry.

There is little doubt that the greatest single gift that you as a parent can give is that of a great reputation and a great work ethic. It has been our pleasure to know many, many clients who have left considerable wealth in the hands of their children and the children have gone on to become quite beneficial to society and great parents to the grandchildren and the great-grandchildren.

Unfortunately, it has also been our experience to witness significant wealth being passed to children who have no appreciation from where it came, no understanding of their place in society and have gone on to wreck and ruin.

It is that in the absence of individuals understanding that there is such a thing as too much money; that is, a gift of money to children particularly those who have received the money through a lottery, through the sale of a business or an inheritance may cause long-term difficulties for that child and for the grandchildren thereon. It is only with planning and in many cases with statements to the children that a significant amount of the family wealth is going to be given away when the parents pass on that the children will start to sweat over their dollars and thereby build a career, establish their own reputation and continue the parents' legacy.

Chapter 21

The Lesson of the Boy Who Cried Wolf

I really want to ensure that this book is not perceived as a quick fix, cookie cutter, all-you-need-to-do, oversimplified, automatic response type piece of work.

I started talking about wisdom in the first chapter and I want to end by talking about judgment.

Judgment is a decision making process where you weigh in all factors.

Maybe a parable will help.

Let's use "The Boy Who Cried Wolf".

The "The Boy Who Cried Wolf" is a tragic tale of a young boy with poor vision of his own future.

The boy was a shepherd; a particularly difficult job where staying awake is a major challenge. After all, one of the biggest parts of the job is counting sheep. The other part was watching out for wolves.

In the event of a wolf sighting, he had to notify the local village people (the residents of the village—not the singing group, although that might have worked out better).

Anyway, the village people would come running at the call of "Wolf" and bring all manner of pitch forks, spears and bow and arrows to prevent the wolf from attacking.

Now this young boy got bored and called out "Wolf" on three separate occasions when, in fact, there was no wolf.

Instead of the village people seeing this as a series of training drills designed to improve their rapid response times and hone their wolf protection strategy, they were very upset and chastised the boy. It did not help when the boy laughed.

You see, if the boy could have held back his laughter he could have developed this business into a consulting service, going from village to village obtaining contracts as a security consultant, eventually making enough money to help fund the campaigns of the local mayors and eventually influence each town council so that he could gradually increase his fees over time and keep out the competition.

But I digress . . . .

Unfortunately, the wolf did show up and the village people heard the boy call out but ignored him. The boy's gene pool was not permitted to continue when he sacrificed himself for his sheep and ended up in the belly of the wolf.

This story is often told to children as a lesson in honesty when parents focus on the consequences of not telling the truth.

But it also serves well here. For another reason.

You see, the wolf did show up.

When we reviewed the newspaper headlines with their dire predictions of further market collapse and expectations of another great depression, it is easy to look at these statements the same as the boy crying wolf when in fact the wolf did not appear.

But we have had the wolf show up a good number of times, just not yet on the Toronto or New York Stock Exchange.

Most recently it showed up in the year 2000 on the NASDAQ market.

And in 1989 in Japan. These are two markets that suffered catastrophic losses and, as of 2011, have still not recovered to their previous highs.

My point is that one should not take the lack of a catastrophe as a sign that a catastrophe will not ever happen. The bailouts that the various governments have instituted over the years have been getting larger and larger but even governments have limits and we may have reached those limits in 2008.

If we as investors do not elect officials who will make real changes to address the growing problem of government deficits the wolf may indeed show up along with a bear market that governments can no longer bail out.

Be informed and ready. Investing wisely is more than just focusing on your current savings. It is about looking at the REALLY BIG PICTURE—how your country itself makes decisions on financial regulation, monetary and fiscal policy.

The next crash may push governments to the limit.

Chapter 22

The Next Roller Coaster Ride

So after 21 chapters, numerous charts, graphs, headlines, statistics, studies and discussions, where does all that leave us?

I hope it leaves you feeling more knowledgeable and empowered.

But let's add one more parable.

In one of the earlier chapters, I discussed how a particular dinosaur ride at Disney World with my five-year-old son really gave me insight as to how investors often feel about the turbulent world of the stock and bond markets.

Well, two years later, we went on another dinosaur ride—this one at a water park at Universal Studios, and this time my wife and mother-in-law accompanied my son and me.

This one was scary too and my son and I were avidly watching my wife and mother-in-law to see their reactions. In comparison, my son and I were relatively calm, well, right up to the seven-story drop and splash down at the end. Both my son and I commented that this ride was nowhere near as scary as the Disney dinosaur ride.

But after thinking about it, maybe it was. It very well may have been just as scary but since my wife and mother-in-law were newbies to dinosaur rides while my now seven year old son and I were veterans, we, the veterans, may have reacted more calmly.

And there is the lesson that I hope you will take away from this book.

As we have seen in previous chapters, the difficulty with investing today relates to the fact that the cycles of boom and bust have been shorter than those in the previous twenty years, the heights of the recoveries and the depth of the falls have been more extreme, and there is a greater sense of uncertainty. Consequently, the simpler rules of the past no longer work and there is an increased requirement for vigilance and flexibility in the use of different tools.

I hope you gleaned some of those tools from this book.

In early 2009, an acquaintance of mine saw that I was giving a lecture in his community titled "When Will The Recession End and Preparing to Prosper". Like many addled investors he commented, "I suppose that you are going to tell us all what we should have done to avoid another 2008 crash."

He was implying that, in hindsight, many advisors know with certainty how to avoid the last market crash. This is like the army generals of World War Two who, after many years of analysis, knew how to fight the battles of World War One.

My staff and I used the strategies in this book to avoid much of the fall of 2008. Further, in making the call to invest aggressively in early 2009, our clients benefitted from the dramatic market rise since then.

This acquaintance of mine was not a client and is not one now and therefore was not aware of our recommendations but obviously is as jaded as many other investors.

We are not trying to tell you how to avoid the last crash. The point is, we will not know about the next crash until it happens but we hope that this book will help identify when the risk of one is highest and when the opportunities that will subsequently arise should be taken advantage of.

There are no perfect investment advisors. However, our business is a lot like the game of horseshoes and the effects of hand grenades—you do not have to make a perfect pitch to make a real difference. You just have to be somewhat close.

A while ago a friend, who is an avid motorcyclist, raved about the joy he receives from riding his bike. I have also met people who would change jobs to get nearer to a salmon fishing river and others who love sailing with a passion, and I am surrounded by golf fanatics and RV nuts.

I do not have any of those passions. I sometimes think I am missing a gene.

I have been on the Gander River, where I was in the middle of telling a joke and hooked a salmon, which promptly went behind a rock, the line got tangled, and I managed to free the line after some cantankering, landed the salmon and saw that the people in the nearby boats almost had a grand mal seizure. When I asked why they looked so wide-eyed they said, "You had a salmon on and nearly lost it!"

I asked them if they remembered the joke. They had not. I was very disappointed.

Another time I was sailing in Newfoundland when I had to use the facilities. We were heaved over at about a 30 degree angle in a 29 foot C&C under heavy sail so aiming for the toilet was a bit of precision work. Just as I successfully finished the boat straightened up from 30 degrees over to level. Essentially, the wall I had been facing rushed up at me and clobbered me full on. Fortunately, I did not hurt anything valuable—only my head. I did, however, in my attempt to gain stability, rip the towel rack completely off the wall.

I returned topside, holding on to said towel rack, and apologized to the owner about the damage, and asked what had happened.

"A lull" was the reply. The lull was the calm before the storm. I had just wrapped my leg around the boat rail when the boat heaved over sharply and I was looking at green water coming over the side as a continuous wall of wind hit us.

We had only been out on the water for one hour before the storm hit. It took us three hours to get back in and at times I wondered what would have happened if one of us had been thrown into the sea. In Newfoundland, you have between 15 to 20 minutes to get out of the water before you die. I am now convinced that life preservers on sailboats in Newfoundland are not designed to save the person you throw the preserver to—it is only used to mark their grave.

So, I do not have the gene to get excited about sailing.

And then there is golf.

I have tried to get excited about golf but in my frustration have found that I sometimes have put too much energy into my swing and, consequently, have become, really, little more than a divot master. I have hit the ground so hard on golf courses sometimes that I have dug up plumbing.

At one golf course a groundskeeper recommended that I add a hoe to my golf bag as one of my most necessary and frequently used clubs.

Talk about humiliation.

I explained to him that I already had a hoe for my golf bag but it was out getting re-gripped.

So, golf does not really do it for me.

What I do get excited about is writing and investing.

Writing allows me to put my thoughts in order.

Lloyd Williams, one of my mentors in this industry, turned to me at a dinner in 2002 and said "You could spend your whole life in your head."

This was not a compliment. He meant that I was too intellectual to be an advisor, that I thought too much about the why of the market and not the how, and that I focused on the theory and not on what was practical.

Investing to me is like a grand puzzle that really, no one has yet to solve fully and it is one of the greatest puzzles of all time. If one can get "more than just close" in this arena, one can so positively affect so many families that it becomes a legacy in itself.

I confess to the fascination and the enthusiasm of investing.

I have studied the history of investing extensively and discovered that we often mistake co-incidence for cause and effect and often ignore other not so obvious factors that may directly affect one's observations.

For example, most of Modern Portfolio Theory was developed during the 1970's and 1980's, a period when markets generally rose and provided positive returns. This was also a time when enforcement of insider trading regulations was less stringent, not necessarily because of intention but more because of the millions of transactions being processed manually. In fact it was only in 1983 that certain insider transactions were made illegal.

Therefore, many people, including regulators, concluded that Modern Portfolio Theory worked because it "explained" how investment managers made great money for clients. But was it possible that many mutual funds gave great returns because the overall markets were rising and some outperformed the markets because they had whispers of insider information during a time when markets generally rose?

We do not know for sure but do know that as enforcement of insider information regulations has increased, and markets have become more volatile, mutual funds have not outperformed the index.

Interesting?

Yes.

We have a passion for investing and will continue to investigate this puzzle in pursuit of a grand, unified theory.

Thank you for reading this.

Appendix A

The True Cost of Fund Ownership

FUND RESEARCH   PRIVATE CLIENT RESEARCH

The Trading Expense Ratio and the Overall Cost of Fund Ownership: 2009 Edition

James Gauthier, CFA / (416) 350-3369
jgauthier@dundeewealth.com

May 22, 2009

It is once again time for our annual peek into the minutiae of mutual fund financial statements to determine just how much some of the country's best known offerings are paying in brokerage commissions. Of course, such an effort is far from being purely academic because ultimately the cost of buying and selling securities is borne by the investors in the fund. Everyone is familiar with the MER, which includes a fund's management fee, operating expenses and GST. Trading expenses – which are a real cost of fund ownership – are not included in the MER.

If you take a fund's MER and add the trading commissions, you come up with the overall cost of fund ownership. We coined this figure the "total expense ratio" in back in 2004 when we first wrote on this subject. At that time, coming up with the total expense ratio was a tedious manual process that involved some fairly liberal assumptions, but about three years ago the regulators mandated that fund companies disclose commission costs and other portfolio transaction costs as an annualized percentage of daily net assets. This figure, which may be found in a fund's MRFP, is called the "trading expense ratio" (TER), and for once we could thank the regulators for making our lives easier. The true cost of fund ownership equals the TER plus the MER.

Not surprisingly, there is a very strong relationship between the level of trading costs and the level of portfolio turnover. Funds that employ a momentum approach tend to have very high levels of turnover, but outside of that, there are not necessarily specific styles that typically have high trading costs. We've seen situations where value, growth and dividend funds have high trading expenses, and other instances where the funds employing the same styles have very limited trading expenses. It is very important to note that in addition to the amount of turnover in a fund, overall trading costs are also a function of the pricing a fund is able to get for its trade execution.

At the end of the day, however, the figure that matters most is performance, and mutual fund return stats are reported net of all fees, including brokerage commissions. All things being equal, funds with lower MERs and brokerage fees will outperform their more expensive counterparts. That said, things are not always equal and a strategy that involves heavy trading is only effective if the manager employing the strategy is consistently able to post strong relative performance. Otherwise, it could be argued that the heavy trading creates a cost hurdle that may be difficult for the manager to overcome and there's no question that funds with consistently high trading expenses and chronic underperformance should be avoided.

For the purposes of this report, we analyzed the largest funds from 16 of Canada's biggest load fund companies to see how significantly trading expenses affected the overall cost of owning the funds. Close to 200 funds were analyzed and the median trading expense ratio was 13 basis points. That's pretty reasonable (and is identical to the median TER from a year ago), and it cannot be forgotten that trading costs are a part of doing business. However, 16% of the funds we looked at had a TER of 30 basis points or higher and 12 products had a TER of 50 basis points or more. Those numbers are meaningful.

Table I: Statistics for the Funds Considered for Most Recent Year-End Statements

	Turnover	MER	TER	Cost of Ownership*	TER/MER
Average	54%	2.42%	0.19%	2.61%	7.9%
Median	38%	2.40%	0.13%	2.59%	5.8%

*MER+TER

Source: Fund company reports, DundeeWealth

Table II highlights the funds with the highest TERs among the offerings we considered. In most instances for this and all other tables in this report, the turnover, MER and TER information is to the most recent fiscal year end for each fund. The quartile information is to April 30, 2009. Although this performance analysis presented in the table is somewhat rudimentary, it can be concluded that the funds that have performed in the top two quartiles of their respective category over one, two and three years have been effective in overcoming their high trading costs. For those funds that have not performed so well, we would argue that high trading costs are not solely responsible for the underperformance, but they certainly haven't helped. Not surprisingly, the median turnover for the funds in Table II during the past year was quite high, coming in at 81%.

Table II: Highest TERs of the Funds Analyzed Plus Relative Performance Data

Fund	Turnover	MER	TER	Cost of Ownership	TER/ MER	1-Yr Quart	2-Yr Quart	3-Yr Quart
Dynamic Power American Growth	564%	2.40%	1.15%	3.55%	48%	4	1	3
CI Cambridge Global Eq	139%	2.39%	0.93%	3.32%	39%	2	-	-
CI Cambridge Cdn Eq	122%	2.41%	0.88%	3.29%	37%	2	-	-
Mac Growth	82%	2.39%	0.80%	3.19%	33%	4	4	4
AGF Dividend Income	361%	2.08%	0.68%	2.76%	33%	4	3	4
AGF China Focus Class	80%	2.96%	0.61%	3.57%	21%	3	2	2
Sprott Cdn Eq	34%	2.81%	0.60%	3.41%	21%	2	3	2
Fidelity Far East Fund Sr B	170%	2.56%	0.59%	3.15%	23%	1	1	1
CI Cambridge Cdn AA	71%	2.43%	0.55%	2.98%	23%	3	-	-
Fidelity Europe Fund Sr B	180%	2.51%	0.55%	3.06%	22%	4	1	1
Mac Universal Canadian Resource	71%	2.43%	0.51%	2.94%	21%	4	3	3
Acuity All Cap 30 Cdn Equity	129%	2.91%	0.50%	3.41%	17%	4	3	2
Mac Universal Precious Metals	35%	2.43%	0.48%	2.91%	20%	4	3	3
CI American Equity	77%	2.31%	0.47%	2.78%	20%	3	4	3
CI Global	58%	2.32%	0.47%	2.79%	20%	3	4	4
Mac Universal European Opps	44%	2.49%	0.47%	2.96%	19%	3	3	4
Brandes Global Small Cap Equity	86%	2.57%	0.45%	3.02%	18%	3	4	4
Mac Universal Int'l Stock	46%	2.45%	0.44%	2.89%	18%	3	1	1
Renaissance Cdn Small Cap	75%	2.49%	0.44%	2.93%	18%	2	2	2
Acuity Growth and Income	148%	2.91%	0.43%	3.34%	15%	4	4	4

Source: Fund company reports, Morningstar

In Short: Successful Investing During Turbulent Times

The funds in Table III have the lowest TERs of the products we looked at. The median level of turnover for the funds in Chart II was 13%, or one-sixth the median turnover level for the funds in Table II

Table III: Lowest TERs of the Funds Analyzed Plus Relative Performance Data

Fund	Turnover	MER	TER	Cost of Ownership	TER/ MER	1-Yr Quart	2-Yr Quart	3-Yr Quart
IA Clarington Canadian Cons. Eq	8%	2.42%	0.02%	2.44%	0.8%	2	1	2
Manulife Monthly High Income	33%	2.09%	0.02%	2.11%	1.0%	2	2	2
AGF Canadian Stock	12%	2.35%	0.03%	2.38%	1.3%	3	2	2
Dynamic Focus + Diversified Income	2%	2.08%	0.03%	2.11%	1.4%	3	3	3
Renaissance Cdn Balanced	14%	2.15%	0.03%	2.18%	1.4%	1	2	2
CI Harbour Fund	10%	2.30%	0.04%	2.34%	1.7%	1	1	1
Fidelity Monthly Income Ser B	24%	2.22%	0.04%	2.26%	1.8%	3	3	2
Trimark Select Canadian Growth	11%	2.34%	0.04%	2.38%	1.7%	4	4	4
AGF Canadian Growth Equity	12%	2.90%	0.05%	2.95%	1.7%	3	3	3
AGF European Eq Class	17%	2.93%	0.05%	2.98%	1.7%	1	4	3
AIC Diversified Canada	9%	2.39%	0.05%	2.44%	2.1%	3	4	4
Bissett Multinational Growth A	17%	2.62%	0.05%	2.67%	1.9%	2	2	2
CI Harbour Growth & Income	10%	2.30%	0.05%	2.35%	2.2%	2	1	1
Fidelity Canadian Balanced Ser B	37%	2.22%	0.05%	2.27%	2.3%	3	1	1
IA Clarington Canadian Dividend	28%	2.69%	0.05%	2.74%	1.9%	2	2	2
IA Clarington Global Equity	20%	2.48%	0.05%	2.53%	2.0%	2	3	3
Mac Balanced	16%	2.68%	0.05%	2.73%	1.9%	3	2	2
Mac Ivy Canadian	22%	2.37%	0.05%	2.42%	2.1%	1	1	3
Templeton Growth	10%	2.30%	0.05%	2.35%	2.2%	3	3	3
Bissett Dividend Income A	12%	2.45%	0.06%	2.51%	2.4%	2	4	4

Source: Fund company reports, Morningstar

The information in Table IV is similar to what's presented in Table II, except rather than displaying the funds with the highest absolute TER, this table presents the funds with the highest TER/MER ratio.

Table IV: Funds with the Highest TER/MER Ratios

Fund	2007 Turnover	2007 MER	2007 TER	Cost of Ownership	TER/MER
Dynamic Power American Growth	564%	2.40%	1.15%	3.55%	48%
CI Cambridge Global Eq	139%	2.39%	0.93%	3.32%	39%
CI Cambridge Cdn Eq	122%	2.41%	0.88%	3.29%	37%
Mac Growth	82%	2.39%	0.80%	3.19%	33%
AGF Dividend Income	361%	2.08%	0.68%	2.76%	33%
Fidelity Far East Fund	170%	2.56%	0.59%	3.15%	23%
CI Cambridge Cdn AA	71%	2.43%	0.55%	2.98%	23%
Fidelity Europe Fund	180%	2.51%	0.55%	3.06%	22%
Sprott Cdn Eq	34%	2.81%	0.60%	3.41%	21%
Mac Universal Canadian Resource	71%	2.43%	0.51%	2.94%	21%
AGF China Focus Class	80%	2.96%	0.61%	3.57%	21%
CI American Equity	77%	2.31%	0.47%	2.78%	20%
CI Global	58%	2.32%	0.47%	2.79%	20%
Mac Universal Precious Metals	35%	2.43%	0.48%	2.91%	20%
Mac Universal European Opps	44%	2.49%	0.47%	2.96%	19%
CI International	45%	2.32%	0.42%	2.74%	18%
Mac Universal Int'l Stock	46%	2.45%	0.44%	2.89%	18%
Renaissance Cdn Small Cap	75%	2.49%	0.44%	2.93%	18%
Brandes Global Small Cap Equity	86%	2.57%	0.45%	3.02%	18%
Dynamic Global Value	30%	2.40%	0.42%	2.82%	18%

Source: Fund company reports, DundeeWealth

The majority of the funds we looked at had reasonable MER/TER ratios. In other words, the TER was rarely a significant part of the overall cost of ownership. Only 23% of the funds we looked at had a ratio in excess of 10% (Chart I), but as Table IV clearly indicates, there were some extreme cases at the high end.

Chart I: MER/TER Ratios Frequency of Funds Considered

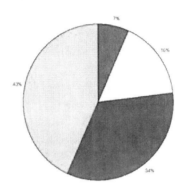

| ■ >20% □ 10% to 20% ■ 5% to 10% □ <5% |

Source: Fund company reports, DundeeWealth

In Short: Successful Investing During Turbulent Times

We felt it would be interesting to provide readers with some sense of just how much large mutual funds typically pay brokerage firms for services. The absolute level of commission dollars paid is of little relevance without considering the size of the fund, but the information in Table V clearly shows that funds with low TERs can still be very lucrative clients for investment dealers.

Table V: Brokerage Commissions Paid by Selected Funds

Fund	Year-End Assets ($000)	MER	TER	Turnover	Brokerage Commissions ($000)
CI Signature Select Canadian	3,886,107	58%	2.30%	0.24%	11,220
Fidelity Northstar	2,458,923	84%	2.44%	0.24%	10,395
Fidelity Canadian Disciplined Equity	1,728,134	159%	2.40%	0.39%	9,849
Trimark Select Growth	2,972,126	76%	2.42%	0.22%	9,104
Mac Universal Canadian Resource	1,878,930	71%	2.43%	0.51%	8,861
Fidelity Canadian Asset Allocation	8,300,761	64%	2.38%	0.10%	8,780
CI Global	1,406,580	58%	2.32%	0.47%	8,573
CI Canadian Investment	5,533,406	17%	2.25%	0.07%	7,247
CI Harbour Growth & Income	6,579,625	10%	2.30%	0.05%	5,728
Fidelity Europe Fund	637,627	180%	2.51%	0.55%	5,392
Trimark Fund	3,031,819	41%	1.80%	0.13%	5,276
AGF Dividend Income	684,286	261%	2.08%	0.68%	5,231
Fidelity True North Fund	4,476,019	39%	2.39%	0.06%	5,037
Mac Cundill Value C	6,316,970	13%	2.42%	0.11%	4,898
CI Signature Income & Growth	2,375,827	49%	2.30%	0.14%	4,245
Trimark Income Growth	4,295,017	50%	1.64%	0.07%	3,998
Mac Growth	452,810	82%	2.39%	0.80%	3,589
Dynamic Power American Growth	286,453	564%	2.40%	1.15%	2,839
Fidelity Far East Fund	354,185	170%	2.56%	0.59%	2,516
Sprott Cdn Eq	1,115,333	34%	2.81%	0.60%	1,871

Source: Company Reports

The Bottom Line

Portfolio managers who employ high turnover strategies rarely change their stripes, and in many cases, an active trading approach defines who a manager is. High turnover tends to lead to high trading costs; therefore, a manager with a consistently high rate of turnover will also tend to have a consistently high TER.

It is nearly impossible for PMs who turn over their portfolios 200%, 300% or more annually to keep the brokerage costs under wraps, but it is certainly possible for a good manager to have a tremendous amount of success by employing a heavy trading strategy. That said, high trading costs create performances hurdles for super-active managers that less active managers don't have to deal with. Additionally, in good times, managers with high turnover strategies are more likely to trigger capital gains, which can lead to taxable distributions to investors. By no means does heavy trading automatically lead to inferior performance, nor does infrequent trading lead to superior performances, but the hurdle that comes with frequent trading and high trading costs is something that advisors and investors should be aware of.

DUNDEEWEALTH

Larry Short

Disclosures & Disclaimers

Glossary

Adjusted Cost Base (ACB): This is what you really paid, including all fees and charges, less any tax breaks or discounts. Be careful here; sometimes there are hidden fees, so ask every "dumb" question you can think of before your next purchase or sale.

Alternative Minimum Tax (AMT): Remember that income tax was a temporary tax brought in to pay for the First World War. Since then there have been a number of attempts to simplify the tax system. This is another one. Even if you obey all the rules to lower your taxes, this is the government's own loophole to get you. So be careful in your tax planning, or you may trigger this tax inadvertently.

Annual Percentage Rate (APR): Remember how you should only compare apples to apples? Well, APR is one way you can have interest rates quoted to you. The other way is Effective Annual Rate (EAR). As long as all quotes are on the same basis, you are fine. In general though, it's always easier to keep an EAR to interest rates.

Annuitant: An annuity pays cash. The annuitant receives the cash.

Annuity: A contract sold by a life insurance company that guarantees a fixed or variable payment for a period of time in the future. This is essentially a long-term Guaranteed Investment Certificate with two key differences—you never get your principal back in one lump sum, and annuities are only available from life insurance companies. It pays you as long as you keep breathing. Variations are available; guaranteed terms, ten-year terms, or joint ownerships. Annuities can be a retirement vehicle to provide the annuitant with a guaranteed income. It can be purchased with either registered (RRSP/RRIF/RPP) or non-registered funds. A prescribed annuity is purchased outside an RRSP or RIF and gives substantial tax breaks.

Arm's Length Transaction: This is necessary where there is a potential for conflict of interest. The transaction is conducted as though the people involved don't know each other. It will affect the price of the transaction and cause the trade to reflect fair market value. It therefore avoids any semblance of a conflict of interest.

Asset: Anything that is worth something, including stocks, bonds, land, trees, car parts, and even "intangible" assets such as goodwill, rights, or things.

Attribution Rules: You cannot put your investments in your minor children or grandchildren's names and have them pay tax at a lower tax rate. You will still be taxed if you do this. It is another way for Canada Revenue Agency to reach out and touch you. The rules cover transfers of property to spouses as well. It also means that those Canada Savings Bonds that Nan gave to her grandchildren will be taxed as if Nan kept them herself. There are few choices here, so a good discussion with your accountant may save you some grief at tax time.

Beneficiary: When you pass on, this person receives your money or other assets.

Beta: Convoluted term meaning risk. The higher the beta, the higher the risk. Not often used by humans, but more easily employed by institutions and pension funds. Can be a bit useful when discussing mutual funds. It is one measure of history that may have no bearing on the future.

Blue Chip Stocks: The stocks of the largest companies listed on the exchange. These companies have a "blue aura" about them because it is believed that their history will continue on into the future. This is not always true, but it is a good place to start.

Bond: A bond is essentially a post-dated cheque that pays interest until a future date, commonly referred to as maturity. A bond is secured which means if the issuer defaults, bondholders immediately get the secured property. A debenture is similar to a bond but it is not secured. All bonds mature at 100 per cent of face value but can sell for more or less than that depending on interest rate levels, the credit rating of the issuer, and the time left until it matures.

Bond Market: This market is actually ten times larger than the stock market but doesn't attract much public attention. Governments put us in debt by borrowing money by issuing bonds. A government bond is a loan to the government. Corporations can also issue bonds. Insurance companies and banks go to this market to buy bonds with the money you deposited with them. You can also go there directly or through mutual funds to get higher interest rates for your investments.

Book Value: The accountant's record of what something cost when it was originally purchased. The selling price today is called market value. Other terms you might hear are salvage value, which is the sacrifice price you would receive if you had to sell it immediately, and appraised value, which is what a professional estimator will tell you it is worth.

Budget: This is your financial road map that details how much money is coming in, what are you spending it on, and how much is left over to save for the future.

Buy-Sell Agreement: This is your legal agreement on how to split up a business partnership.

Canada Savings Bonds (CSBs): One type of government bond issued by Ottawa, CSBs are sold once a year. They are issued at par value (100 per cent) and can be cashed at any time at par (plus the accrued interest) at many financial institutions. They are not marketable and cannot be traded. This means that you cannot earn capital gains on them. CSBs are available in regular interest form, with the accumulated interest paid with the principal when the bond matures.

Capital Gain (Loss): The profit or loss resulting from the sale of a capital asset, such as bonds, stock, or real estate. Fifty per cent of capital gains are tax-free. Tax is paid on the balance of 50 per cent of the gain at the investor's marginal tax rate. This means that the most you would pay in tax on a capital gain of $100.00 would be about $21.70 (assuming a marginal tax rate of 43.4%). This is better than the maximum you would pay in tax on interest income of $100, which is about $43.40.

Capitalization: Market price of shares x number of outstanding shares. Gives an idea of how big a company is. "Small Cap Stocks" have a lower value than "Large Cap Stocks." Often, Large Cap Stocks are called "Blue Chip Stocks."

Cash Value or Cash Surrender Value (CSV): The cash value that develops in a whole life insurance policy. It belongs to the insurer, but is accessible to the policyholder as a loan or as a refund on cancellation of the policy. It forms a part of the death benefit.

Certified Financial Planner (CFP®): Internationally recognized educational accreditation for financial planners, administered under the Financial Planning Standards Council™. There are also Registered Financial Planners (R.F.P.®), Chartered Financial Planners (a designation from the UK), and Personal Financial Planners (PFP®). Interview your planner to see if he/she has one of these designations.

Comprehensive Financial Plan: A written document that addresses all the elements of a financial plan in an integrated manner. It covers both short-term, medium-term, and long-term objectives. Essentially, it is your financial road map. Without such a map, you have no idea where you are going. With a plan, you may be able to save on taxes and sleep better at night with better certainty of the future.

Current Yield: This is the annual income from an investment expressed as a percentage of the investment's current market price. Be careful when it comes to long-term bonds or bond funds, because the current yield can be misleading there.

Deemed Disposition: A term used to describe the motions of selling or buying a particular investment as the investor is "deemed" to have bought or sold the investment. From Canada Revenue Agency's point of view, this action triggers a capital gain or loss even if the physical investment is not sold. When you die, Canada Revenue Agency believes that you sold everything just as you passed away, which triggers taxes to your estate.

Diversification: Spreading the risk of an investment portfolio by investing in different asset classes (cash, bonds, and stocks), in different types of investments within each asset class (from conservative to aggressive), and in different markets (in both Canada and international markets), in order to minimize excessive exposure to any one source of risk. Too often this is overlooked in order to "win big," which is often the reason why people lose big.

Dividend Tax Credit: A special tax credit that reduces the amount of tax levied on dividends paid to individual taxpayers by Canadian corporations. It is how you get your piece of the action and get a tax break as well. Makes investing in utility and bank stocks very interesting.

Dividends: The direct payments public corporations make to their shareholders on a pro-rata basis. An investor can receive dividend income from preferred and common shares. This is your portion of the profits of the companies you invest in.

Dow Jones Industrial Average (The Dow): The major stock barometer in the U.S., it is a price-weighted average of thirty actively traded "blue chip" stocks. These stocks are worth about one-quarter of the value of all stocks on the New York Stock Exchange, and represent the major industrial sectors of the economy. It is the most widely reported U.S. stock index. Be careful though, because the Dow can fall while other stocks rise. Another more accurate measure is the S&P 500 (see following).

Equities: Just another more technical and confusing name for stocks or shares.

Estate: What you own when you die or when you are incapacitated or bankrupt and your financial and legal affairs are being overseen by a legally appointed representative.

Executor/Executrix: Person or corporation appointed by you in your Will to carry out the instructions in your will. It is a big job, so choose very carefully.

Fair Market Value: What something can sell for today if you are not in a hurry. If you are in a hurry, it may be best to look at Salvage Value.

Fixed-Income Securities: Bonds, preferred shares, and Guaranteed Investment Certificates. Annuities may also fall into this category.

Growth Stocks: Stock of corporations that have exhibited faster-than-average gains in profits over the last few years. They tend to be in companies in fast-growing areas such as high tech or pharmaceuticals.

Guaranteed Investment Certificate (GIC) and Term Deposits: Securities sold by banks, trust companies, and credit unions that pay interest for deposits (from thirty days to five years). The Canadian Deposit Insurance Corporation (CDIC) covers GIC deposits at banks and trust companies for amounts up to $100,000. The amount of credit union insurance coverage differs by province.

Income Attribution: This is Canada Revenue Agency's way of preventing you from moving money into the hands of someone who pays a lower tax than you. Be careful here. Putting money in your children's hands may still mean you have to pay the tax, perhaps with a penalty. Consult a tax professional when in doubt.

Income Splitting: Shifting taxable income from a taxpayer with a higher marginal tax rate to a taxpayer with a lower marginal tax rate, while avoiding the attribution rule.

Intestate: An individual dying without a will. Then the will the government writes for you prevails and you might not be too happy with that. You could end up paying more taxes under the government will.

Joint and Last Survivor Annuity: An annuity contract that covers more than one person and promises to pay periodic payments until the death of the last surviving person covered.

Leverage: The strategy of borrowing funds to invest. The hope is that the investment will earn a greater rate of return than the after-tax cost of borrowing. The risk is that the investment will fall in value.

Liabilities: What you owe.

Life Income Fund (LIF): In the past, if you transferred from a company and took a Locked-in RRSP, you had to transfer the money to an annuity to actually get cash in your hands. Now you can transfer a LIF, which gives you more flexibility. LIF terms tend to differ from province to province.

Life Insurance: A contract that pays money on the death of the insured person to a named beneficiary or to the deceased's estate.

Locked-in RRSP/LIRA: A retirement account that allows you to move your Registered Pension Plan from a company you worked for to an RRSP when changing jobs.

Maturity Date: The date on which an investment or a mortgage comes due.

Money Market: Guaranteed investments that mature within one year.

Mortgage-backed Security (MBS): A security that consists of a pool of residential mortgage loans backed by the federal government under the National Housing Authority (NHA). Purchasers receive payments of both interest and principal on the underlying mortgages, usually monthly.

Mutual Funds: A corporation or a trust, that pools the money of many investors and employs a professional investment manager. The fund manager purchases a collection of stocks, bonds, or other securities to meet the fund's objective, which is outlined in a document called a prospectus.

Open-ended Mutual Fund: This is a type of mutual fund we generally are used to hearing about. It is the opposite of a closed-ended fund. In an open-ended fund shares (sometimes called units) are issued and redeemed according to investor demand. The mutual fund company buys or sells the shares, which do not trade on a stock exchange. Shares are purchased or sold at their Net Asset Value (NAV).

Over-the-Counter (OTC): Securities that trade on an over-the-counter basis do not trade on a listed exchange. Both the money market and the bond market are examples of OTC markets.

Owner, Life Insurance: The person who pays the premiums of the insurance policy. The owner can be the insured, his/her employer, the beneficiary, or other third parties. If you buy life insurance on your spouse, you are the owner and your spouse is the insured. The owner of the policy must have an insurable interest in the life insured.

Pension Income Tax Credit: A federal tax credit meaning that you do not pay tax on the first $1,000 of eligible pension income you receive.

Portfolio: A combination of stocks, bonds, and cash for the purpose of reducing risk through diversification.

Preferred Shares: Non-voting shares that usually pay dividends at a fixed rate. These shares have preferential status over common shares, meaning that their owners are paid first from any profits and, in the event of bankruptcy, are paid back before the common shareholders. There are different types of preferred shares.

Prescribed Annuity: An annuity that is prescribed by the *Income Tax Act*. Consequently, the income received from it is taxed at a lower rate than normal. Therefore, you end up with more money from this than from bonds or GICs. But be careful. This only works outside an RRSP or RIF and may only continue for as long as you do, leaving nothing to your heirs. Some do have guarantees.

Registered Pension Plan (RPP): A pension plan put together by your employer. Contributions by employees reduce their taxable income. Similar to an RRSP, income earned in the plan accumulates tax-free as long as the funds remain in the plan.

Registered Retirement Income Fund (RRIF): Used to "mature" your RRSP. A minimum amount must be withdrawn on an annual basis once the plan is set up, and that money is taxed as income as you receive it. The remaining money in the plan continues to earn income tax-free. The latest date for the transfer of RRSP assets into a RRIF is at age 71.

Registered Retirement Savings Plan (RRSP): A plan registered with Canada Revenue Agency that enables tax-sheltered retirement savings. A reduction in taxable income is earned when a contribution to an RRSP is made. Investment income earned within the plan is not taxed. However, tax is paid upon the withdrawal of funds. An RRSP matures when the owner turns 71 and must be: 1) rolled to a RRIF; 2) rolled to an annuity; 3) withdrawn in its entirety (and tax paid on the entire withdrawal amount: this is not an advisable option in most cases).

Risk: The probability of an investment falling so that you lose money. The higher the probability of negative rate of return, the higher the risk of the investment.

Risk/Return Trade-off: Generally, the higher the risk, the higher the return on an investment.

Segregated Fund: A mutual fund run and managed by a life insurance company. A guarantee of at least 75 per cent of the deposits, less any withdrawals, is provided at the earlier of the death or agreed-upon maturity date of the plan. These funds can be invested in a wide range of asset types and are becoming quite popular. They operate under different rules and regulations than non-segregated mutual funds.

Shareholder: Individual or organization owning shares in a corporation. Also known as a stockholder or equity owner.

Small Cap (Capitalization) Stocks: Shares of a publicly traded company with a small market capitalization. A small cap stock usually has a market capitalization of no greater than $500 million in the U.S. In Canada the definition is more loose but generally means the smaller companies listed on a stock exchange.

Spousal RRSP: A Registered Retirement Savings Plan in which the contributions are made and the tax deduction is taken by one spouse and the plan is owned by the other spouse. This is great for long-term income splitting.

Standard & Poor's 500 (S&P 500): The S&P 500 is similar to the Dow 30 but is a more broad-based indicator of the U.S. stock market. It is based on the average performance of five hundred widely held "large cap" stocks in the U.S.

Stock Market: Marketplace where buyers and sellers trade stocks (also known as shares or equities). Stocks can be those of larger, well-known public corporations or smaller, less-well-known firms. Stocks can be of the following types, as well as others: preferred shares, common shares, and closed-end mutual funds.

Strip Bond: Also known as a "Zero Coupon Bond" (see following).

Tax Avoidance: The act of reducing taxes in ways that are legal. Often thought of as using "tax loopholes," really just rearranging your affairs to take advantage of provisions of the *Income Tax Act* that allow you to lower your tax bill.

Tax Evasion: The illegal act of failing to accurately report income or failing to pay taxes.

Tax Shelter: An investment that has significant tax savings, such as immediate tax deductions or credits. Be careful here.

Tax-free Rollovers: A direct transfer of funds from a company pension plan or other tax sheltered plans into an RRSP or RRIF. Unfortunately, it is not as wonderful as it sounds, because all you are doing is moving the money from one account where tax is not being paid to another where tax is not being paid. In any case, you will be taxed when you withdraw money from the original or the final account.

Term Life Insurance: Life insurance that is in force for a specific period or term, as long as you keep up with the payments.

Treasury Bill (T-Bill): A short-term government promissory bond that has a maturity of 91, 182, or 364 days.

Underwriting: The process whereby an insurance company determines whether to accept you as a client. In the case of life and health insurance, this would apply to health of the applicant, financial status, personal habits, occupation, and many other factors that could have an impact on the likelihood of you dying earlier than usual.

Universal Life Insurance: A type of permanent life insurance in which the owner places cash (single or ongoing premiums) into a deposit account with the insurance company. The insurance company withdraws the necessary funds from the account to keep the life insurance in force. The remaining funds in the deposit account remain the property of the policyholder and are paid at death in addition to the specified death benefit. Investment return on that money accumulates tax-free unless withdrawn prior to the death of the insured person. This allows this plan to act as a tax shelter to some degree.

Whole Life: A type of permanent life insurance in which all cash values are owned by the insurance company and form a part of the death benefit of the policy.

Will: A legal document that expresses an individual's instructions on how to distribute his or her estate after death.

Zero Coupon Bonds: Bonds are issued with coupons attached that entitle the holder to receive interest payments if they hold them on a certain date. A bond can be "stripped" of its coupons. Then both the stripped bond (the residual) and its coupons are sold separately. Both the residual and coupons pay no periodic interest but are priced at below their face value. The difference between the purchase price and the current market value is deemed to be interest for tax purposes.

CPSIA information can be obtained at www.ICGtesting.com
Printed in the USA
LVOW080218060312

271765LV00001B/1/P